Guiding Those Left Behind
In Virginia
2nd Edition

LEGAL AND PRACTICAL THINGS
YOU NEED TO DO
TO SETTLE AN ESTATE IN VIRGINIA
and
HOW TO ARRANGE YOUR OWN AFFAIRS
TO AVOID UNNECESSARY COSTS
TO YOUR FAMILY

By AMELIA E. POHL, ESQ.

with Virginia Attorney
STEPHEN J. KAUFMANN

 EAGLE PUBLISHING COMPANY OF BOCA

The purpose of this book is to provide the reader with an informative overview of the subject; but laws change frequently and are subject to different interpretations as courts rule on the meaning or effect of a law. This book is sold with the understanding that neither the publisher nor the authors are engaging in, nor rendering legal, accounting, medical, psychiatric, financial planning or any other professional service. If you need legal, accounting, medical, psychiatric, financial planning or other expert advice, then you should seek the services of a licensed professional.

WEB SITES: Web sites appear throughout the book. These Web sites are offered for the convenience of the reader only. Publication of these Web site addresses is not an endorsement by the authors, editors or publishers of this book.

This book is intended for use by the consumer for his or her own benefit. If you use this book to counsel someone about the law, or tax matters, then that may be considered to be an unauthorized and illegal practice.

EAGLE PUBLISHING COMPANY OF BOCA
4199 N. Dixie Highway, #2
Boca Raton, FL   33431
E-mail   info@eaglepublishing.com

Printed in the United States of America
ISBN 1-892407-25-6
Library of Congress Catalog Card Number: 2001116239

The Organization of the Book

If you are going to GUIDE THOSE LEFT BEHIND, you need to know what is involved in settling an estate in Virginia, so we begin the book explaining that process. The first six chapters explain:

1. How to tend to the funeral and burial
2. What agencies need to be notified of the death
3. How to locate the decedent's property
4. What bills need (and do not need) to be paid
5. Determining who are the beneficiaries
6. Getting the decedent's property to the proper beneficiary

We devoted a chapter to each of these 6 steps; and for those who are in the process of settling an estate, we placed a CHECK LIST at the end of Chapter 6 summarizing the many things that need to be done.

Once you read Chapters 1 through 6 you will be able to identify those problems that can occur when someone dies. Using those Chapters as a base, the rest of the book (Chapters 7 through 11) explain how you can set up your own Estate Plan so that your family is not burdened by similar problems.

GLOSSARY

This book is designed for the average reader. Legal terminology has been kept to a minimum. There is a glossary at the end of the book in the event you come across a legal term that is not familiar to you.

FICTITIOUS NAMES AND EVENTS

The examples in this book are based loosely on actual events; however, all names are fictitious; and the events, as portrayed, are fictitious.

ACKNOWLEDGMENT

When someone dies, the family attorney is often among the first to be called. Family members have questions about whether probate is necessary, who to notify, how to get possession of the assets, etc. Over the years, as we practiced in the field of Elder Law, we noticed that the questions raised were much the same family to family. We both agreed that a book answering such questions would be of service to the general public.

We also observed, that those who had experience in settling the estate of a loved one had an understanding of the process, and were better able to make decisions about their own estate plan. We decided to combine the two topics: Settling An Estate and Estate Planning into a single book *Guiding Those Left Behind*. We wish to thank all of the clients, whom we have had the honor and pleasure to serve, for providing us with the impetus to produce this book.

SPECIAL THANKS FROM AMELIA E. POHL
I wish to thank my brothers Paul and Fred Adinolfi, my sister Nancy Simonyi, my daughters Louise Lucas and Margo Bosche, and my husband J. William Pohl. Working on this series of books was just that much easier because of the support given to me by all the members of my family.

SPECIAL THANKS FROM STEPHEN J. KAUFMANN
My sincere gratitude to my wife and team partner, Bonnie L. Kaufmann. Through her background as an insurance and business consultant, and in construction, and generally a "taking care of business" person, she has provided invaluable help, support and encouragement in this effort. I also dedicate this book to my clients who in their estate planning have made life much simpler for "those left behind in Virginia."

About The Author

Before becoming an attorney in 1985, AMELIA E. POHL taught mathematics on both the high school and college level. During her tenure as Associate Professor of Mathematics at Prince George's Community College in Maryland, she wrote several books including Probability: A Set Theory Approach, Principals of Counting and Common Stock Sense.

During her practice of law Attorney Pohl observed that many people want to reduce the high cost of legal fees by performing or assisting with their own legal transactions. Attorney Pohl found that, with a bit of guidance, people are able to perform many legal transactions for themselves. Attorney Pohl utilizes her background as teacher, author and attorney to provide that "bit of guidance" to the general public in the form of self-help legal books that she has written. Attorney Pohl is currently "translating" this book for the remaining 49 states:

Guiding Those Left Behind in Colorado
Guiding Those Left Behind in Connecticut, etc.

Consulting Virginia Attorney

STEPHEN J. KAUFMANN is noted nationally for his dedication to helping people protect their assets, privacy and quality of life as an Elder Law and Estate Planning attorney. He is an educator and nationally known author of many estate planning books and educational courses in the Legal-Financial Estate Planning and Insurance industry. He has been noted in Newsweek, published in Financial Planning, US News and World Report, Life Association News (LAN-Now Advisor), Life Insurance Selling, Broker World and appears often in national publications. He has over 25 years experience in Elder Law and Estate Planning and is the former Deputy Commissioner of Insurance, Virginia State Corporation Commission.

Steve practices through his law firm - ABC LAW, and serves families, farm and small business owners throughout Virginia and works with other attorneys, financial, insurance and other professionals and their clients nationally. He is a humorous and educational public speaker for many local and national conferences.

Steve presents programs on radio, television, and national educational forums. He has spoken before U.S. Congressional and state legislative committees and was responsible for writing the laws on Long Term Care and other insurance products as the former Virginia Deputy Insurance Commissioner. He is the President and Founder of The Estate Planning Institute and the professional designation Study program, CEPP, Chartered Estate Planning Practitioner.

Steve is a member of the National Academy of Elder Law Attorneys, past president of the Central Virginia Chapter of Chartered Life Underwriters. He is also a member of the International Association of Financial Planners and former Chairperson for Federal and State Legislative Committee, Virginia Association of Insurance and Financial Advisors. He is the founder of the Kaufmann Foundation, a charitable organization that provides educational programs to the public and gifts to programs that inspire, educate and help people protect their quality of life around the world.

Steve has been in private and government practice since 1974. He graduated from Boston College (MBA) in 1970, and from Suffolk University Law School in 1974.

Steve and his wife Bonnie Kaufmann, an instructor and insurance-life style and business consultant have five sons ranging in ages from 17 to 30. They live in Luray, Virginia. Together they present the radio program "Law and Your Money©" that is aired on different radio stations. You can find the time and location of their next radio broadcast at their Web site:

http://www.abclaw.com

Guiding Those Left Behind In Virginia
CONTENTS

Reading the Law

Where applicable, we identified the state statute or federal statute that is the basis of the discussion. We did this as a reference, and also to encourage the general public to read the law as it is written. Prior to the Internet the only way you could look up the law was to physically take yourself to the local courthouse law library or the law section of a public library. Today all of the state and federal statutes are literally at your finger tips. They are just a mouse click away on the Internet. To look up the statute all you need is the address of the Web site and the identifying number of the statute:

 FEDERAL STATUTE WEB SITE
http://www4.law.cornell.edu/uscode
VIRGINIA STATUTE WEB SITE
http://www.state.va.us

Virginia has compiled their laws into some 66 Titles. For example INSURANCE is Title 38 (as well as 38.1 and 38.2), HEALTH is 32.1. WILLS AND DECEDENTS' ESTATES' 64.1, and so on. We will identify the statute by the number of the title and the section within that title. For example (VA 64.1-69.1). To look up this statute, you go to the statute section of the Web site and then to the Table of Contents to Title 64.1 and then to section 69.1. An easier method is to type 64.1-69.1 in the "Search" box.

If you come across a topic in the book that is important to you, then you may find it both interesting and profitable to actually read the law as written.

About The Book

We tried to make this book as comprehensive as possible so there are specialized sections of the book that do not apply to the general population and may not be of interest to you. The following GUIDE POSTS appear throughout the book. You can read the section if the situation applies to you or skip the section if it doesn't.

GUIDE POSTS

The SPOUSE POST means that the information provided is specifically for the spouse of the decedent. If the decedent was single, then skip this section.

The CALL-A-LAWYER POST alerts you to a situation that may require the assistance of an attorney. See page xiii for information about how to find a lawyer.

The CAUTION POST alerts you to a potential problem. It is followed by a suggestion about how to avoid the problem.

The SPECIAL SITUATION POST means that the information given in that paragraph applies to a particular event or situation; for example when someone dies a violent death. If the situation does not apply in your case then you can skip the section.

When You Need A Lawyer

The purpose of the book is to give the reader a basic understanding of what needs to be done when someone dies, and to provide information about how a person can arrange his own affairs to avoid problems for his own family. It is not intended as a substitute for legal counsel or any other kind of professional advice. If you have any legal question, then you should to seek the counsel of an attorney. When looking for an attorney, consider three things: EXPERTISE, COST and PERSONALITY.

EXPERTISE

The state of Virginia does not have a program to certify that an attorney is specialized in a particular area of law. However, attorneys are allowed to state that they are certified by an accredited institution, if such is the case. For example, the National Elder Law Foundation has a certification program for the field of Elder Law. An attorney certified by the Foundation, or other program such as being a Chartered Estate Planning Practitioner is allowed to make that fact known to the public.

There is a Lawyer Referral Service located in each county Bar Association. They can refer you to an attorney in your area who practices the type of law that you seek. You can get the number of the Lawyer Referral Service in your county by calling the State Bar of Virginia at (800) 552-7977. You can get information about the State Bar Referral Service at their Web site:

 VIRGINIA STATE BAR WEB SITE
http://www.vsb.org/

One of the most reliable ways to find an attorney is through personal referral. Ask your friends, family or business acquaintances if they used an attorney for the field of law that you seek and whether they were pleased with the results. It is important to employ an attorney who is experienced in the area of law you seek. Your friend may have a wonderful Estate Planning attorney, but if you suffered an injury to your body, then you need an attorney experienced in Personal Injury.

Before employing an attorney for a job, ask how long he has practiced that type of law and what percentage of his practice is devoted to that type of law.

COST

In addition to the attorney's experience, it is important to check what it will cost in attorney's fees. When you call for an appointment ask what the attorney will charge for the initial consultation and the approximate cost for the service you seek. Ask whether there will be additional costs such as filing fees, accounting fees, expert witness fees, etc.

If the least expensive attorney is out of your price range then you can call your local county Bar Association for the telephone number of the Legal Aid office nearest you.

The American Bar Association has a directory of Virginia Legal Services Programs at the General Public Resources section of its Web site:

 AMERICAN BAR ASSOCIATION WEB SITE
http://www.abanet.org

PERSONALITY

Of equal importance to the attorney's experience and legal fees, is your relationship with the attorney. How easy was it to reach the attorney? Did you go through layers of receptionists and legal assistants before being allowed to speak to the attorney? Did the attorney promptly return your call? If you had difficulty reaching the attorney, then you can expect similar problems should you employ that attorney.

Did the attorney treat you with respect? Did the attorney treat you paternally with a "father knows best" attitude or did the attorney treat you as an intelligent person with the ability to understand the options available to you and the ability to make your own decision based on the information provided to you.

Are you able to understand and easily communicate with the attorney? Is he/she speaking to you in plain English or is his/her explanation of the matter so full of legalese to be meaningless to you?

Do you find the attorney's personality to be pleasant or grating? Sometimes people rub each other the wrong way. It is like rubbing a cat the wrong way. Stroking a cat from head to tail is pleasing to the cat, but petting it in the opposite direction, no matter how well intended, causes friction. If the lawyer makes you feel annoyed or uncomfortable, then find another attorney.

It is worth the effort to take the time to interview as many attorneys as it takes to find one with the right expertise, fee schedule and personality for you.

The First Week 1

Dealing with the death of a close family member or friend is difficult. Not only do you need to deal with your own emotions, but often with those of your family and friends. Sometimes their sorrow is more painful to you, than what you are experiencing yourself.

In addition to the emotional impact of a death, there are many things that need to be done, from arranging the funeral and burial, to closing out the business affairs of the *decedent* (the person who died) and finally giving whatever property is left to the proper beneficiary.

The funeral and burial take only a few days. Wrapping up the affairs of the decedent may take considerably longer. This chapter explains what things you (the spouse or closest family member) need to do during the first week, beginning at the moment of death and continuing through the funeral.

 MALE GENDER USED

Rather than use "he/she" or "his/her" for simplicity
(and hoping not to offend anyone)
we will refer to the decedent and his
Personal Representative using the male gender.

References to other people will be in both genders.

AUTOPSIES

In today's high tech world of medicine, doctors are fairly certain of the cause of death, but if there is a question, the doctor may seek permission to perform an autopsy. Virginia statute establishes an order of priority to authorize the procedure:

1st   Anyone authorized by the decedent, in a signed, notarized writing, to dispose of his body.

2nd The spouse   3rd An adult son or daughter

4th   Either parent   5th An adult brother or sister

6th   A court appointed guardian of the decedent

7th   Anyone authorized to dispose of the body

No authorization can be made if someone with the same or higher priority object to the examination (VA 54.1-2825, 54.1-2973). The person giving authorization must agree to pay for the autopsy because the cost is not covered under most health insurance plans. An autopsy can cost anywhere from several hundred to well over three thousand dollars, but it is in the family's best interest to consent to the autopsy. The examination might reveal a genetic disorder, that could be treated if it later appears in another family member. Death from a car "accident" could have been a heart attack at the wheel. Perhaps the patient who died suddenly in a hospital was misdiagnosed. The nursing home resident could have died from negligence and not old age. Even if none of these are found, knowing the cause of death with certainty is better than not knowing.

That was the case with the family of a woman who was taken to the hospital complaining of stomach pains. The doctors thought she might be suffering from gallbladder disease but she died before they could effectively treat her. A doctor suggested that an autopsy be performed to determine the actual cause of death. The woman had three daughters, one of whom objected to the autopsy: "Why spend that kind of money? It won't bring Mom back."

The daughter's wishes were respected, however over the years as they aged and became ill with their own various ailments they would undergo physical examinations. As part of taking their medical history, doctors routinely asked "And what was the cause of your mother's death?" None could answer the question.

This is not a dramatic story. No mysterious genetic disorder ever occurred in any of her daughters, nor in any of their children. But each daughter (including the one who objected) at some point in her life, was confronted with the nagging question "What did Mom die of?"

MANDATORY AUTOPSIES

When a person dies, a physician must sign the death certificate stating the cause of death. If a person dies in a hospital, then there is a doctor present to sign the certificate. If a person who was not under the care of a physician, dies suddenly at home, or if someone dies through accident, foul play or suicide, then the police must be notified. The person who discovers the body should call 911 to summon the police. The police will ask the county Medical Examiner to determine the cause of death. The Medical Examiner will have an autopsy performed whenever there is a suspicion that the death was not from natural causes or that the death was caused by a disease that could pose a threat to the public health (VA 32.1-263, 32.1-283).

AUTOPSIES PERFORMED BY THE INSURANCE COMPANY:

A company that issues an accident or sickness insurance in the state of Virginia is required to have the policy include a statement that the company has the right to perform an autopsy (VA 38.2-3503). The cost of the autopsy is paid for by the insurance company, so they will not order an autopsy unless there is some important reason to do so.

ANATOMICAL GIFTS

If, before death, the decedent made an anatomical gift by signing a donor card or by giving his Health Care Agent authority to make the gift as part of a Advance Medical Directive, then hospital personnel or the donor's doctor need to be made aware of the gift in quick proximity to the time of death — preferably before death.

The federal government has established regional Organ Procurement Organizations throughout the United States to coordinate the donor program. There are two Organ Procurement Organizations located in Virginia: LifeNet in Virginia Beach and the Washington Regional Transplant Consortium located in Falls Church, Virginia. If the hospital staff thinks that a patient may be a candidate for a donation, they will contact these organizations.

The Organ Procurement Organization will make an assessment and determine whether the patient is a suitable donor. Early on in the donor program those over 65 were not considered as suitable candidates. Today, however, the condition of the organ, and not the age, is the determining factor. If the Organ Procurement Organization decides to request the gift, then someone who is specially trained will approach the family to request permission for the donation.

If the decedent appointed a Health Care Agent and gave the Agent authority to make the donation, then the Agent can give permission.

If no Agent was appointed, then Virginia statute gives an order of priority for giving permission for the donation:

1st   Spouse   2nd   Adult son or daughter
3rd Either parent   4th   An adult brother or sister
5th   A grandparent
6th   The decedent's court appointed guardian (if any)

When permission is obtained from a family member and there are others in the same or a higher priority, then an effort must be made to contact those people and make them aware of the proposed gift. For example, if the sister of the decedent agrees to the gift (4th in priority) and the decedent had an adult child (2nd in priority), then the child needs to be made aware of the gift. If the child objects, then no gift can be made. Similarly, the statute prohibits the gift if, just before he died, the decedent said he did not want to make a donation (VA 32.1-290.1).

AFTER THE DONATION

Once the donation is made the body is delivered to the funeral home and prepared for burial or cremation as directed by the family. The donation does not disfigure the body so there can be an open casket viewing if the family so wishes.

For privacy reasons, the identity of the donor and the recipient of the gift is not disclosed, but on request from the donor's or recipient's family, most Organ Procurement Organizations will give basic demographic information such as the age, sex, marital status, number of children and occupation of the donor or recipient of the gift.

GIFT FOR EDUCATION OR RESEARCH

The State of Virginia has a State Anatomical Program. The Commissioner of the Program coordinates donations for the purpose of education or research. If a donation is accepted, the Supervision will have the body transported to a medical school. If the medical schools do not have a need for the body, then the Commissioner can make the donation to any school in the Commonwealth authorized to teach health science. Any body not needed by schools within the Commonwealth can be donated to colleges and schools in other states and the District of Columbia (VA 32.1-298, 32.1-299).

If the decedent signed a donor card indicating his wish to use his body for any purpose and he is not a candidate for an organ donation, then you can offer to release the body to the State Anatomical Program, for the purpose of education or research by calling (804) 786-2479.

Bodies that have been embalmed are not suitable for study, so you need to call the school within 24 hours after the death to determine whether the Commissioner will accept the body. The donation will probably be refused if the decedent was extremely obese, or died from a contagious disease or from crushing injuries.

There is no charge to the family for making the gift. The school pays to transport the body to the place of study. It usually takes 18 months to 2 years to complete the study. Once the study is complete, the remains are cremated and the ashes buried at a local cemetery. If the family wishes, the *cremains* (cremated remains) can be returned to the family (VA 32.1-301).

CAVEAT: With the exception of hair, ova, blood and other body fluids (such as sperm cells), it is illegal for anyone to purchase body parts (VA 32.1-289.1). It is legal to charge monies to prepare, store or transport bodies or body parts. Not-for profit and as well as for-profit companies have sprung up that are in the business of preparing, storing and delivering body parts. These companies request donations from families (so they are not buying body parts). The company prepares the body tissue or other parts of the body, and then distributes the parts throughout the United States to physicians, hospitals, research centers, etc. In many cases the monies charged for preparation and transportation includes a sizable profit.

If someone other than a representative of one of the Organ Procurement Organizations identified on page 4 ask you for a donation, then before agreeing, you may want to learn about the company making the request.

What is the name of the company?
Where are their main headquarters located?
What is their primary business activity?
What is the name and job description of the person making the request?

DETERMINE THE END USE OF THE DONATION

You may want to ask what they intend to do with the tissue or body part. If it is being used for research, then what type of research? Where is the research being conducted? If it will be used for transplantation, then what agency (doctor, hospital) will receive the donation and where is that agency located?

Once you have this information you can make an informed decision as to whether you wish to make the donation.

THE FUNERAL

Approximately ten percent of deaths occur suddenly because of accident, suicide, foul play or undetected illness. But, mostly, death occurs after a lengthy illness, with a common scenario being that of an aged person who dies after being ill for several months, if not years. In such case, family and friends are emotionally prepared for the happening. Expected or not, the first job is the disposition of the body.

THE PREARRANGED FUNERAL

Increasingly, people are arranging, in advance, for their own funeral and burial. This makes it easier on the family both financially and emotionally. All the decisions have been made and there is no guessing what the decedent would have wanted.

If the decedent made provision for his burial, then you should come across a burial certificate, or perhaps a deed to a burial space. If he made provision for his funeral, then you should find a Preneed funeral contract. You need to read the contract to determine what provisions were made. If the contract was paid by installment, then you need to determine whether it is paid in full. You also need to determine whether the contract was a fixed price agreement or whether there could be additional charges.

If you cannot locate the contract, but you know the decedent made provision for his funeral, then call the funeral home and ask them to send you a copy of the contract. If you believe the decedent purchased a funeral plan but you do not know the name of the funeral home, then call the local funeral homes. Many local funeral homes are owned by national firms with computer capacity to identify people who have purchased a contract in any of their many locations.

Once you have possession of the contract, take it with you to the funeral home and go over the terms of the contract with the funeral director. Inquire whether there is any charge that is not included in the contract.

MAKING FUNERAL ARRANGEMENTS

If the decedent died unexpectedly or without having made any prior funeral arrangements, then your first job is to choose a funeral director and make arrangements for the funeral or cremation. Most people choose the nearest or most conveniently located funeral home without comparison shopping. However prices for these services can vary significantly from funeral home to funeral home. Savings can be had if you take the time to make a few phone calls.

Receiving price quotes by telephone is your right under Federal law. Federal Trade Commission ("FTC") Rule 453.2 (b) (1) requires a funeral director to give an accurate telephone quote of the prices of his goods and services. Funeral homes are listed in the telephone directory under FUNERAL DIRECTORS. If you live in a small town, there may be only one or two listings. If such is the case, then check out some funeral homes in the next largest city.

Funeral Directors usually provide the following services:
➤ arrange for the transportation of the body
    to the funeral home and then to the burial site
➤ arrange for the embalming or cremation of the body
➤ arrange funeral and memorial services
    and the viewing of the body
➤ order copies of the death certificate for the family
➤ have memorial cards printed
➤ obtain information for the death certificate and file the
    death certificate with the Registrar (VA 32.1-263).

To compare prices you will need to determine:
✧ what is included in the price of a basic funeral plan
✧ whether you can expect any additional cost.
If the decedent did not own a burial space, then that cost must be included when making funeral arrangements.

It may be necessary to have the body embalmed if you are going to have a viewing. Embalming is not necessary if you order a direct cremation or an immediate burial without a viewing. Federal Trade Commission Rule 453.5 prohibits the funeral home from charging an embalming fee unless you order the service.

PURCHASING THE CASKET

When comparison-shopping, you will find that the single most expensive item to be a casket. When selecting a casket you need to be aware that there may be a considerable mark-up in the price quoted by the funeral director. You do not need to go "sole source" when purchasing the casket. If you feel that the price quoted by the funeral director is too high, you can purchase the casket elsewhere and have it delivered to the funeral home to be used instead of the one offered by the funeral director. Federal regulations require a funeral home to accept a casket that is purchased elsewhere.

The funeral director must provide you with a written price list at the beginning of your discussion of funeral arrangements (VA 54.1-2812). If the price list given to you by the funeral home states that the price of their casket includes a specific dollar amount for basic services, and you do not purchase the casket from the funeral home, then the funeral director is allowed to add that specific dollar amount to the charge for his basic services. He is not allowed to charge a handling fee for accepting a casket that is purchased elsewhere (FTC Rule 453.2, 453.4).

Of course the problem with purchasing a casket is that most of us have no idea what to pay. Caskets are not usually displayed for sale in a shopping mall, so how do you determine the going price? The answer is the Internet. You can learn all about the cost of any item, even a casket, by using your search engine to find a retail casket sales dealer. If you are not computer literate, you can locate the nearest retail casket sales outlet by looking in the yellow pages under CASKETS. You may need to look in the telephone directory for the nearest large city to find a listing. By making a call to a retail casket sales dealer, you will become knowledgeable in the price range of caskets. You can then decide what is a reasonable price for the product you seek.

The best time to do your comparison shopping, is before you go to the funeral home to arrange for the funeral. Once you have determined what you should pay for the casket, it is only fair to give the funeral director the opportunity to meet that price. If you cannot reach a meeting of the minds, then you can always order the casket from the retail sales dealer and have it delivered to the funeral home.

ON-LINE FUNERAL SERVICES

The Internet is changing the way the world does business, and the funeral industry is no exception. A growing number of mortuaries are offering live Webcasts of funerals and wakes for those who are unable to pay their respects in person.

There are Web sites such as ObitDetails.com where you can post an obituary. There are on-line memorial chat rooms as well as online eulogies and testimonials. There is even a Web site that offers a posthumous e-mail service which allows people to leave final messages for friends and relatives.

THE CREMATION

Increasingly people are opting for cremation. The reasons for choosing cremation are varied, but for the majority, it is a matter of finances. The cost of cremation is approximately one-sixth that of an ordinary funeral and burial. A major saving is the cost of the casket. No casket is necessary for the cremation and Federal law prohibits a Funeral Director from saying that a casket is required for a direct cremation (FTC Rule 453.3 (b)ii). You may need a suitable container to deliver the body to the crematory. After the cremation, you will need an urn for the ashes.

If you are having a memorial service in a place of worship and no viewing of the body before the cremation, then consider contracting with a facility that does cremations only. Look in the telephone book CREMATION SERVICES. You will also see cremation "societies" in the telephone book. Some are for-profit and others non-profit. You can also find advertisements for cremation services on the Internet.

THE OVERWEIGHT DECEDENT
If the decedent weighs more than 300 pounds, then you need to check to see if the Cremation service has facilities large enough to handle the body. If you cannot locate a crematory that can accommodate the body, then you will need to make burial arrangements.

THE DECEDENT WITH A PACEMAKER
Cremating a body with a pacemaker or any radiation producing devise can cause damage to the cremation chamber or to the person performing the cremation. If the decedent was wearing such electronic aid, then you need to investigate the cost of having it removed prior to the cremation. The Cremation service may be able help you to arrange for the removal of the device.

DISPOSING OF THE ASHES

The decedent's cremains can be placed in a cemetery. Many cemeteries have a separate building called a **columbarium**, which is especially designed to store urns. The cremains can also be placed in a cemetery plot. Some cemeteries allow the cremains of a family member to be placed in an occupied family plot. Similarly, some cemeteries will allow the cremains to be placed in the space in a mausoleum that is currently occupied by a member of the decedent's family. If it is your desire to have the cremains placed in an occupied mausoleum or family plot, then you need to call the cemetery and ask them to explain their policy as it relates to the burial of urns in occupied sites.

If the cremains are to be placed in a cemetery, then you need to obtain a suitable urn for the burial. You can purchase the urn from the Funeral Director or Crematory Service Director. Urns cost much less than caskets, but they can cost several hundred dollars. You may wish to do some comparison shopping by calling a retail sales casket dealer.

ABANDONED CREMAINS

It is important to pick up the cremains after the cremation. If you do not do so, then after 90 days, the funeral director can dispose of them in any manner he sees fit, such as:

- ➤ scattering them at sea or by air
- ➤ placing them in a scatter garden
- ➤ burial of the cremains

The funeral director has the right to charge all costs and reasonable expenses of the final disposition to the person who contracted to have the decedent cremated (VA 54.1-2808.1).

If the decedent is to be buried in another state, then the body will need to be transported to that state. Most funeral homes belong to a national network of funeral homes, and the out-of-state Funeral Director has the means to make local arrangements to ship the body. Contact the out-of-state Funeral Director and have him/her make arrangement with the airline for the transportation of the body. If services are to be held in Virginia and in another state, then your local funeral director can make arrangements with the out-of-state funeral home for the transportation of the body.

TRANSPORTING CREMAINS

If the body has been cremated, then you can transport the cremains yourself, either by carrying the ashes as part of your luggage or by arranging with the airline to transport the ashes as cargo. Have a certified copy of the death certificate available in the event that you need to identify the remains of the decedent.

In these days of heightened security, it is important to call the airline before departure and ask whether they have any special regulation or procedure regarding the transportation of human ashes.

SPOUSE	THE MILITARY BURIAL

Subject to availability of burial spaces, an honorably discharged veteran and/or his unmarried minor or handicapped child and/or his un-remarried spouse may be buried in a national military cemetery. Some cemeteries have room only for cremated remains or for the casketed remains of a family member of someone who is currently buried in that cemetery, so you need to call for space availability.

There are several military cemeteries in Virginia. You will need to call to determine whether space is available. You can call the Culpeper National Cemetery at (540) 825-0027 for space availability at:

>Alexandria National Cemetery at Alexandria
>Balls Bluff National Cemetery at Leesburg
>Culpeper National Cemetery at Culpeper
>Staunton National Cemetery at Staunton
>Winchester National Cemetery at Winchester.

You can call the Fort Harrison National Cemetery at (804) 795-2031 for space availability at:

>City Point National Cemetery at Hopewell
>Cold Harbor National Cemetery at Mechanicsville
>Fort Harrison National Cemetery at Richmond
>Glendale National Cemetery at Richmond
>Richmond National Cemetery at Richmond
>Seven Pines National Cemetery at Sandston

The Department of the Army is in charge of the Arlington National Cemetery. You can call them at (703) 695-3250 for information about having a veteran buried in the Arlington National Cemetery.

Special Situation	THE COST OF A MILITARY BURIAL

Burial space in a National Cemetery is free of charge. Cemetery employees will open and close the grave and mark it with headstone or grave marker without cost to the family. The local Veteran's Administration ("VA") will provide the family with a memorial flag. The family needs to make funeral arrangements with a funeral firm and have them transport the remains to the cemetery.

Regardless of where an honorably discharged veteran, is buried, allowances may be available for the plot, and burial and grave marker expenses. The amount varies depending on factors such as whether the veteran died because of a service related injury. The VA will not reimburse any burial or funeral expense for the spouse of a veteran.

For information about reimbursement of funeral and burial expenses you can call the VA at (800) 827-1000.

The Department of Veteran's Affairs has a Web site with information on the following topics:

> ➤ National and Military Cemeteries
> ➤ Burial, Headstones and Markers
> ➤ State Cemetery Grants Program
> ➤ Obtaining Military Records
> ➤ Locating Veterans

 VA CEMETERY WEB SITE
http://www.cem.va.gov

BENEFITS FOR SPOUSE OF DECEDENT VETERAN

SPOUSE

The surviving spouse of an honorably discharged veteran should contact the Veteran's Administration to determine whether he/she is eligible for any benefits. For example, if the decedent had minor or disabled children, his spouse may also be eligible for a monthly benefit of Dependency and Indemnity Compensation ("DIC"). If the Veteran's surviving spouse receives nursing home care under Medicaid, then the spouse might be eligible for monthly payments from the VA.

Whether a surviving spouse is eligible for any of these benefits depends on many factors including whether the decedent was serving on active duty, whether his death was service related, and the surviving spouse's assets and income. DIC benefits are discontinued should the surviving spouse remarry; however, a recent change in the law permits payments to be resumed, should the subsequent marriage end because of death or divorce.

For information about whether the surviving spouse is eligible for any benefit related to the decedent's military service call the VA at (800) 827-1000. You can receive a printed statement of public policy: VA Pamphlet 051-000-00217-2 FEDERAL BENEFITS FOR VETERANS AND DEPENDENTS by sending a check in the amount of $5 to

THE SUPERINTENDENT OF DOCUMENTS
P.O. Box 371954
Pittsburgh, PA 15250-7954

Information is also available at the VA Web site:

VA WEB SITE
http://www.va.gov

CRIME VICTIM COMPENSATION

A family member or anyone who was living with a deceased victim of a crime may be eligible for compensation under Virginia's COMPENSATING VICTIMS OF CRIME ACT. The state can provide compensation for reasonable funeral expenses (up to $3,500); psychological counseling (up to $1,000 for family members of a homicide), crime scene cleanup (up to $1,000); moving expenses (up to $500). The total compensation may not exceed $15,000.

To be eligible the following must be true:
➢ The crime was reported to authorities within 120 hours of its commission or discovery of the body.
➢ The person seeking compensation (the applicant) has cooperated with law enforcement agencies.
➢ Application for compensation was filed within one year from the injury or death.

You can have an application mailed to you by calling (800) 552-4007 or writing to:
CRIMINAL INJURIES COMPENSATION FUND
WORKERS' COMPENSATION COMMISSION
11513 Allecingie Parkway
Richmond, VA 23235

There are Crime Victims' Ombudsmen who can help you fill out the application and collect necessary documentation to complete your application. You can get the telephone number of the Ombudsman nearest you from your local law enforcement agency or you can call the above 800 number (VA 19.2-368.2, 19.2-368.3:1,19.2-368.4, 19.2-368.5, 19.2-368.10, 19.2-368.11:1).

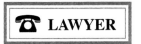 **LAWYER**

THE VIOLENT OR WRONGFUL DEATH

If the decedent died a violent death or under circumstances in which foul play is suspected, the Medical Examiner will take possession of the body. The body will not be released to the funeral director until the examination of the body is complete. In the interim, the family can proceed with arrangements for the funeral. The funeral director will contact the Medical Examiner to determine when he can pick up the body and proceed with the funeral.

THE WRONGFUL DEATH

If the decedent died because of a wrongful act, then the decedent's Personal Representative can sue on behalf of the decedent's Estate, unless, of course, the decedent accepted settlement for the injury before he died. The Personal Representative will use monies recovered to pay attorney's fees and costs, and the decedent's medical and funeral expenses. Whatever is left will be distributed according to the verdict or settlement of the case (VA 8.01-50, 8.01-54).

The Virginia Statute of Limitation for wrongful death is 2 years from the date of death, provided the injury that finally caused the death, happened within the two years before his death. If the initial injury happened more than two years prior to the death, the Personal Representative will not be able to sue for a wrongful death (VA 8.01-244).

If the accident was related to the decedent's job, the family may wish to consult with an attorney who is experienced in Worker's Compensation as well as one experienced in Personal Injury.

If a person dies unattended, the police will try to locate the family. If they cannot identify the body or if his family is unable or unwilling to arrange for his burial, then whoever is in charge of the body (medical examiner, funeral directors, etc.) is required to offer the body to the Commissioner of Virginia's State Anatomical Program to be sent to a medical school for the purpose study or the advancement of science. If the Commissioner refuses the donation, then the sheriff of the county or city where the death occurred will arrange for a cremation or burial.

If the indigent was in a state correctional facility, and his family does not take responsibility for the burial, then the Department of Corrections will offer the body to the Commissioner for the advancement of science. If the Commissioner refuses the donation, then the Department of Corrections will arrange for the cremation or burial(VA 32.1-288).

THE INDIGENT VETERAN
If the indigent decedent was an honorably discharged veteran, the federal government will provide a free burial space and monies may be available to pay for the burial and grave marker as well (see page 16).

 **THE MISSING BODY**

Few things are more difficult to deal with than a missing person. The emotional turmoil created by the "not knowing" is often more difficult than the finality of death. The legal problems created by the disappearance are also more difficult than if the person simply died. It may take a two-part legal process — the appointment of a Conservator to manage his property while he is missing, and then the Probate procedure after the Probate Court has issued an order that the missing person is presumed to be dead.

APPOINTING A CONSERVATOR

If a person is missing and cannot be found after a diligent search, then that person is referred to as an ***Absentee***. If the Absentee has business matters that need attending (bills that need to be paid, checks that need to be cashed, etc.), then anyone who might have an interest in his Estate were he dead (including his creditors) can **petition** (ask) a Judge of the Circuit Court to have a Conservator appointed to manage the absentee's property under court supervision. You will need an attorney experienced in Probate matters to get the Conservatorship established (VA 26-68).

BEGINNING THE PROBATE PROCEDURE

The Probate procedure can begin after:
⇨   The Court rules that there is sufficient evidence to presume that the absentee is dead - or -
⇨   Six months, if the absentee is lost at sea - or -
⇨   7 years have passed.
(VA 64.1-104.5, 64.1-105, 64.1-105.2).

THE PROBLEM
FUNERAL OR BURIAL

The funeral and burial industry is well regulated by both state and federal government. Under Virginia law the following acts are subject to disciplinary action:

☒ Delivering goods of a lesser quality that is presented to the purchaser as a sample

☒ Using a false or misleading advertisement

☒ Paying kick-backs to generate business

☒ Using indecent or obscene language in the presence of a dead body, or within the hearing of the family

☒ Conviction of any felony or any crime involving immoral behavior.

(VA 54.1-2806).

Funeral directors are licensed professionals so it is unusual to have a problem with the funeral or burial or cremation. However, if you had a bad experience with any aspect of the funeral then you can file a complaint with the state licensing agency:

Department of Health Professions
Board of Funeral Directors and Embalmers
6606 W. Broad Street, 4th Floor
Richmond, VA   23230-1717
Telephone (804) 662-9907
In state toll free number (800) 533-1560

 **LAWYER** In addition to filing a complaint with the Board, you may wish to consult with an attorney who is experienced in litigation matters to learn of any other legal remedy that you may have.

THE DEATH CERTIFICATE

It is the job of the Funeral Director or Cremation Service Director to provide information about the decedent to the Vital Records Unit of the Virginia Department of Human Resources. The Vital Records Unit will prepare a death certificate based on that information. It is important that the information you give to the Funeral or Cremation Director is correct. It is also important that you check the form completed by the Funeral or Cremation Director to be sure names are correctly spelled and dates correctly written. Once information is submitted to Vital Records, it will be difficult and time consuming to make a correction.

The Funeral or Cremation Director will order as many certified copies of the death certificate as you request. Most establishments require an original certified copy and not a photocopy so you need to order sufficient certified copies. The following is a list of institutions that may want a certified copy:

* Each insurance company that insured the decedent or his property (health insurance company, life insurance company, car insurance company, home insurance company)
* Each financial institution in which the decedent had money invested (brokerage houses, banks)
* The decedent's pension fund
* Each credit card company used by the decedent
* The IRS
* The Social Security Administration
* The Department of Motor Vehicles
* If a Probate procedure is necessary, then the Clerk of the Circuit Court.

ORDERING COPIES OF THE DEATH CERTIFICATE

Some airlines and car rental companies offer a discount for short notice, emergency trips. If you have family flying in for the funeral, you may wish to order a few extra copies of the death certificate so that they can obtain an airline or car rental discount.

If you wish to order certified copies of the death certificate at a later date, you can call the funeral director and ask him to do so or you can write to:

OFFICE OF VITAL RECORDS AND HEALTH STATISTICS
STATE HEALTH DEPARTMENT
P.O. Box 1000
Richmond, VA 23218-1000

You can make your personal check or money order payable to the State Health Department. The current charge is $8 for each certified copy of the death certificate. You can call (804) 225-5000 for a recorded message that will verify the fee.

About Probate

Once a person dies, all of the property he owns as of the date of his death is referred to as the **decedent's Estate.** If the decedent owned property that was in his name only (not jointly or in trust for someone) then some sort of court procedure is necessary to determine who is entitled to possession of the property. The name of the court procedure is **Probate.**

In Virginia, Probate is conducted in the Circuit Court. The Clerk of the Circuit Court, or the Deputy Clerk of the Circuit Court has authority to conduct the Probate procedure. The one exception is the Probate of the Estate of a person presumed to be dead. In that case, the Probate procedure in conducted under the supervision of a Judge of the Circuit Court (VA 64.1-77, 64.1-107, 64.1-108).

The root of the word Probate is "to prove." It refers to the first step in the Probate procedure, that is, to examine proof of whether the decedent left a valid Will. The next step is to appoint someone to wrap up the affairs of the decedent — to pay any outstanding bills and then to distribute what property is left to the beneficiaries.

If the decedent left a valid Will naming someone as **Executor** of his Estate, then the Clerk will appoint that person for the job. If the decedent died without a Will, the Clerk will appoint someone to be the **Administrator** of the Estate. For simplicity we will refer to the person appointed by the court to settle the decedent's Estate as the **Personal Representative** (VA 55-34.1).

The Clerk will issue a certificate of qualification to the Personal Representative authorizing him to administer the Estate. A copy of the order in which the certificate is granted is usually sufficient to conduct the Probate procedure. If the Personal Representative wishes, he can ask the Clerk to have the Judge issue **Letters**, under the seal of the Court, giving the Personal Representative authority to act (64.1-122). Instead of distinguishing between the certificate of qualification and the Letters, we will refer to the document that authorizes the Personal Representative to act as his Letters.

There are different ways to conduct a Probate procedure depending on the value of the property that is being Probated. We will refer to property that is distributed as part of a Probate procedure as the decedent's **Probate Estate** and the method of conducting a Probate procedure as the **Estate administration**. Chapter 6 explains the different kinds of Estate administration that are available in Virginia.

But we are getting ahead of ourselves. First we need to determine whether a Probate procedure is necessary. To answer that question we need to know exactly what the decedent owned, so the next two chapters explain how to identify, and then locate, all of the decedent's assets.

Giving Notice Of The Death 2

Those closest to the decedent usually notify family members and close friends by telephone. The funeral director will arrange to have an obituary published in as many different newspapers as the family requests, but there is still the job of notifying the government and people who were doing business with the decedent. If no probate procedure is necessary, the job of notifying people of the death falls to his spouse; and in the absence of a spouse, to the decedent's next of kin. By *next of kin,* we mean those people who inherit the decedent's property according to the VIRGINIA'S LAWS OF DESCENT. Those laws are explained in Chapter 5.

If a Probate procedure is necessary then the job of notifying people of the death belongs to the person named as the Executor in the decedent's Will. If the decedent died without a Will, then whoever is appointed as Personal Representative has the job. A majority of the beneficiaries can elect someone to serve as Personal Representative. If there is a disagreement about who should serve, then the Clerk of the Probate Court will make the decision. If there is a surviving spouse, the Clerk will give priority to the spouse (VA 64.1-118).

The person who has the job of settling the decedent's Estate should begin to give notice as soon as is practicable after the death. Two government agencies that need to be notified are the Social Security Administration and the IRS. This chapter gives their telephone number and the telephone number of other agencies that need to be notified.

NOTIFYING SOCIAL SECURITY

Many Funeral Directors will, as part of their service package, notify the Social Security Administration of the death. You may wish to check to see that this has been done. You can do so by calling (800) 772-1213. If you are hearing impaired call (800) 325-0778 TTY. You will need to give the Social Security Administration the full legal name of the decedent as well as his social security number and date of birth.

 *Special Situation*

DECEDENT RECEIVING SOCIAL SECURITY CHECKS

If the decedent was receiving checks from Social Security, then you need to determine whether his last check needs to be returned to the Social Security Administration.

Each Social Security check is a payment for the prior month, provided that person lives for the entire prior month. If someone dies on the last day of the month, then you should not cash the check for that month. For example, if someone dies on July 31st, then you need to return the check that the agency mails out in August. If however, the decedent died on August 1st then the check sent in August need not be returned because that check is payment for the month of July.

If the Social Security check is electronically deposited into a bank account, then notify the bank that the account holder died and notify the Social Security Administration as well. If the check needs to be returned, then the Social Security Administration will withdraw it electronically from the bank account. You will need to keep the account open until the funds are withdrawn.

SPOUSE SPOUSE/CHILD'S SOCIAL SECURITY BENEFITS

If the decedent had sufficient work credits, the Social Security Administration will give the decedent's widow(er) or if unmarried, then the decedent's minor children, a one-time death benefit in the amount of $255.

SURVIVORS BENEFITS:

The spouse (or ex-spouse) of the decedent may be eligible for Survivors Benefits. Benefits vary depending on the amount of work credits earned by the decedent; whether the decedent had minor or disabled children; the spouse's age; how long they were married; etc. The minor child of the decedent may be eligible for benefits regardless of whether the child's father (the decedent) ever married the child's mother. Paternity can be established by any one of several methods including the father acknowledging his child in writing or verbally to members of his family. For more information you can call the Social Security Administration at (800) 772-1213.

SOCIAL SECURITY BENEFITS

A spouse or ex-spouse can collect social security benefits based on the decedent's work record. This value may be greater than the spouse now receives. It is important to make an appointment with your local Social Security office and determine whether you as the spouse (or ex-spouse) or parent of decedent's minor child are eligible for any Social Security or Survivor benefit. The Social Security Administration has a Web site from which you can down load publications that explain survivors benefits:

 SOCIAL SECURITY WEB SITE
http://www.ssa.gov

DECEDENT WITH GOVERNMENT PENSION

Any pension or annuity check received after the date of death of a federal retiree, or a survivor annuitant, needs to be returned to the U.S. Treasury. If the check is direct deposited to a bank account, then call the financial institution and ask them to return the check. If the check is sent by mail then you need to return it to:

Director, Regional Finance Center
U. S. Treasury Department
P.O. Box 7367
Chicago, IL 60680

Include a letter explaining the reason for the return of the check and stating the decedent's date of death.

$$$ APPLY FOR BENEFITS $$$

A survivor annuity may be available to a surviving spouse, and/or minor or disabled child. In some cases, a former spouse may be eligible for benefits. Even though you notify the government of the death, they will not automatically give you benefits to which you may be entitled. You need to apply for those benefits by notifying the Office of Personnel Management ("OPM") of the death and requesting that they send you an application for survivor benefits. You can call them at (888) 767-6738 or you can write to:

THE OFFICE OF PERSONNEL MANAGEMENT
SERVICE AND RECORDS CENTER
BOYERS, PA 16017

You will find brochures and information about Survivor's Benefits at the OPM Web site:

OFFICE OF PERSONNEL MANAGEMENT WEB SITE
http://www.opm.gov

DECEDENT WITH A COMPANY PENSION OR ANNUITY

In most cases, pension and annuity checks are payment for the prior month. If the decedent received his pension or annuity check before his death, then no monies need be returned. Pension checks and/or annuity checks received after the date of death may need to be returned to the company. You need to notify the company of the death to determine the status of the last check sent to the decedent.

Before notifying the company, locate the policy or pension statement that is the basis of the income. That document should tell whether there is a beneficiary of the pension or annuity funds now that the pensioner or annuitant is dead. If you cannot locate the document, use the return address on the check envelope and ask the company to send you a copy of the plan. Also request that they forward to you any claim form that may be required in order for the survivor or beneficiary to receive benefits under that pension plan or policy.

If the pension/annuity check is direct deposited to the decedent's account, then ask the bank to assist you in locating the company and notifying the company of the death.

DECEDENT WITH AN IRA or
QUALIFIED RETIREMENT PLAN ("QRP")

Anyone who is a beneficiary of an Individual Retirement Account ("IRA") or QRP needs to keep in mind that, in general, no income taxes have been paid on monies placed in an IRA or QRP account. Once monies are withdrawn, significant taxes may be due. You need to learn what options are available to you as a beneficiary of the plan and the tax consequences of each option. You will need to ask an accountant how much will be due in taxes for each option. Once you know all the facts, you will be able to make the best choice for your circumstance.

SPOUSE

If the spouse is the beneficiary of the decedent's IRA account, then there are special options available. The spouse has the right to withdraw the money from the account or roll it over into the spouse's own retirement account. Although the employer can explain options that are available, the spouse still needs to understand the tax consequence of choosing any given option. It is important to consult with an accountant to determine the best way to go.

If the decedent had a QRP, the plan may permit the spouse to roll the balance of the account into a new IRA. The spouse needs to contact the decedent's employer for an explanation of the plan and all the options that are available at this time.

NOTIFYING IRS

THE FINAL INCOME TAX RETURN

The decedent's final income tax return (IRS form 1040) needs to be filed by April 15th of the year following the year in which he died. The state income tax is filed at the same time (VA 58.1-341). If the decedent was married, then the surviving spouse can file a final joint return. If there is no surviving spouse, then it is the Personal Representative's job to file the final income tax return.

If no Probate procedure is necessary, then whoever inherits the decedent's property needs to file the final return. If you have a joint bank account with the decedent, you may want to keep the account open until you determine whether the decedent is entitled to an income tax refund. See Chapter 6 for an explanation of how to obtain a refund.

THE GOOD NEWS

Monies inherited from the decedent are generally not counted as income to you, so you do not pay federal income tax on those monies. If the monies you inherit later earn interest or income for you, then of course you will report that income as you do any other type of income.

┃ SPOUSE ┃ ▶ SELLING THE HOMESTEAD

In the tough "ole days" the IRS used to allow capital gains tax exclusion (up to $125,000) on the sale of one's homestead (the principal residence). A person had to be 55 or older to take advantage of the exclusion, and it was a once-in-a-lifetime tax break. If a married couple sold their home and took the exclusion it was "used up" and no longer available to either partner.

In these, the good times, the IRS allows you to sell your homestead and up to $250,000 ($500,000 for a married couple) of the home-sale profit is tax free (IRC Section 121(b) 3). There is no limit on the number of times you can use the exclusion, provided you own and live in the homestead at least two years prior to the sale.

If, under the old law, the decedent and his spouse used their "once in a lifetime" homestead tax exclusion, with this new law, the surviving spouse can sell the homestead and once again take advantage of a tax break.

AN ESTATE TAX FOR THE WEALTHY

The *Taxable Estate* of the decedent is the total value of all of his property, as of his date of death. This includes real property (homestead, vacant lots, etc.) and personal property (cars, life insurance policies, business interests, securities, IRA accounts, etc.). It includes property held in the decedent's name alone, as well as property that he held jointly or in trust for another.

An *Estate Tax* is a tax imposed by the federal and state government for the transfer of property at death. There is a federal *Gift Tax* on gifts given during a person's lifetime that exceed $10,000 per person, per year. Should a gift be given that exceeds $10,000, that gift must be reported to the IRS, but no tax need be paid unless the total value of gifts made in excess of $10,000 previously made by that person, exceeds a certain amount as set by the government. Once a person dies the cumulative value of gifts reported to IRS in excess of $10,000 per year is added to the decedent's Taxable Estate. No federal Estate Tax need be paid unless the combined sum exceed the exclusion amount as set by the federal government. This amount is scheduled to increase as follows:

YEAR	EXCLUSION AMOUNT
2002-2003	$1,000,000
2004-2005	$1,500,000
2006-2008	$2,000,000
2009	$3,500,000

There is an unlimited marital tax deduction for property transferred to the surviving spouse; so in most cases, no Estate Tax need be paid if the decedent was married. Regardless of whether taxes are due, federal and state Estate Tax returns must be filed whenever the decedent's Estate exceeds the exclusion amount in effect as of his date of death (VA 58.1-901, 58.1-902).

The current federal Estate Tax is scheduled to be phased out in the year 2010, but a new Capital Gains Tax is scheduled for 2010 that may prove even more costly than the Estate Tax. The new Capital Gains Tax is related to the way inherited property is evaluated by the federal government. Real and personal property is inherited at a "step up" in basis. This means that if the decedent purchased an item that is worth more than when he purchased it, the beneficiary will inherit the property at its fair market value as of the decedent's date of death. For example, if the decedent bought stock for $20,000 and it is worth $50,000 as of the date of death, his beneficiary will take a step-up in basis of $30,000, meaning that the beneficiary inherits the stock at the $50,000 value. If the beneficiary sells the stock for $50,000, he pays no Capital Gains tax. If the beneficiary holds onto the stock and later sells it for $60,000, the beneficiary will pay a Capital Gains tax only on the $10,000 increase in value since the decedent's death.

Up to 2009, there is no limit to the amount you can take as a step-up in basis. But in 2010 caps are set in place. The decedent's Estate will be allowed a 1.3 million dollar step-up in basis, plus another 3 million for property passing to the surviving spouse. The new law could result in significant Capital Gains taxes that the beneficiary must pay. For example, suppose in 2010 you inherit a business from your father that he purchased for $100,000 and it is now worth 2 million dollars. There is a Capital Gain of 1.9 million dollars, but you are allowed a step-up in basis of only 1.3 million. Should you decide to sell the business, $600,000 of your inheritance will be subject to a Capital Gains tax.

No one knows how the new law will be applied in 2010, but it could well be that the Capital Gains tax on your inheritance turns out to be the same as, if not more than, what you would have paid in Estate Taxes, before they were "phased out."

THE UN-UNIFIED GIFT TAX
As explained on page 36, the Gift Tax is unified with the Estate Tax so that if you give a gift to someone in excess of $10,000, the amount over $10,000 is added to your Taxable Estate. Up until the change in the law, you did not need to pay a Gift Tax during your lifetime unless the amount given during your lifetime exceeded the exclusion amount. That changes in 2004. In 2004, the exclusion amount for the Estate Tax goes up to $1,500,000, but the exclusion amount for the Gift Tax remains at $1,000,000.

Specifically, if you make a gift to anyone of more than $10,000 per year, the amount over $10,000 must be reported to the IRS. The IRS keeps a running count of the reported values. As of 2004, once the sum of all of your reported values exceed $1,000,000, you will pay a Gift Tax on any amount that you give during your lifetime that exceeds $10,000 per person per year.

The Estate Tax is scheduled to be repealed in 2010, but not the Gift Tax.

THE PROBATE ESTATE TAX

Virginia has a tax of 10 cents per $100 of value of the decedent's Probate Estate (see page 140). No tax is due if the Estate is $10,000 or less (VA 58.1-1712).

DECEDENT WITH A TRUST

If the decedent was the Grantor (or Settlor) of a Trust, then he was probably managing the Trust as Trustee during his lifetime. The Trust document should name a **Successor Trustee** to manage the Trust now that the Grantor is deceased. The Trust document may instruct the Successor Trustee to make certain gifts once the Grantor dies or the Trust document may direct the Successor Trustee to hold money in trust for a beneficiary of the Trust.

IF YOU ARE SUCCESSOR TRUSTEE

If you are the Successor Trustee then in addition to following the terms of the Trust, you are required to obey all of the laws of the state of Virginia relating to the administration of the Trust. You should consult with an attorney experienced in Estate Planning to help you administer the Trust according to the law and without any liability to yourself.

IF YOU ARE A BENEFICIARY

If you are a beneficiary of the Trust, then you may want to employ your own attorney to explain your rights in the Trust. For example, if you do not live in Virginia, you have the right to require that the Trust assets, or any part of it, be moved to your state. If the Successor Trustee does not live in your state, then you have the right to request that a Trustee from your state be appointed to manage the Trust property (VA 26-64, 26-66).

NOTIFYING THE BUSINESS COMMUNITY

People and companies who were doing business with the decedent need to be notified of his death. This includes utility companies, credit card companies, banks, brokerage firms and any company that insured the decedent. Examine the decedent's financial records to determine the name and telephone number of all of the companies that insured the decedent or his property. Look for all kinds of insurance policies, including real property insurance, motor vehicle insurance, health insurance and life insurance.

MOTOR VEHICLE INSURANCE

Locate the insurance policy for all motor vehicles owed by the decedent (car, truck, boat, airplane; and notify the insurance company of the death. Determine how long insurance coverage continues after the death. Ask the insurance agent to explain what things are covered under the policy. Is the motor vehicle covered for all types of casualty (theft, accident, vandalism, etc.) or is coverage limited in some way?

If you can continue coverage, then determine when the next insurance payment is due. Hopefully, the car will be sold or transferred to a beneficiary before that date, but if not, you need to arrange for sufficient insurance coverage during the Probate procedure.

NOTIFY LIFE INSURANCE COMPANIES

You need to determine whether the decedent life insurance, and if so, then you need to locate the policy and notify the company of his death. Call each life insurance company and ask what they require in order to forward the insurance proceeds to the beneficiary. Most companies will want the original policy and a certified copy of the death certificate.

Send the original policy by certified mail or any of the overnight services that require a signed receipt for the package. Make a copy of the original policy for your records before mailing the original policy to the company.

IF YOU CANNOT LOCATE THE COMPANY

If you cannot locate the insurance company it may be doing business under another name or it may no longer be doing business in the state of Virginia. Each state has a branch of government that regulates insurance companies doing business in that state. If you are having difficulty locating the insurance company call the Department of Insurance in the state where the policy was purchased and ask for assistance in locating the company. In Virginia, the number for the Bureau of Insurance is (804) 371-9741. In state, you can call (800) 552-7945.

EAGLE PUBLISHING COMPANY OF BOCA has the telephone number for the Department of Insurance for each state at their Web site:

 EAGLE PUBLISHING COMPANY OF BOCA WEB SITE
http://www.eaglepublishing.com

IF YOU CANNOT LOCATE THE POLICY

If you know that the decedent was insured, but you cannot locate the insurance policy, you can contact the company and request a copy of the policy. A tougher question is how to locate the policy if you can't find the policy and do not know the name of the insurance company. The American Council of Life Insurers offers suggestions that you may find helpful at the Missing Policy Inquiry page of their Web site:

AMERICAN COUNCIL OF LIFE INSURERS WEB SITE
http://www.acli.com

Special Situation

ACCIDENTAL DEATH

If the decedent died as a result of an accident, then check for all possible sources of accident insurance coverage including his homeowner's policy. Some credit card companies provide accident insurance as part of their contract with their card holders.

If the decedent died in an automobile accident, check to see whether he was covered by any type of travel insurance, such as rental car insurance. If he belonged to an automobile club, such as AAA, then check whether he had accident insurance as part of his club membership.

HOMEOWNERS' INSURANCE

If the decedent owned his own home, then check whether there is sufficient insurance coverage on the property. The decedent may have neglected to increase his insurance as the property appreciated in value. If you think the property may be vacant for some period of time, then it is important to have vandalism coverage included in the policy. Once the property is sold, or transferred to the proper beneficiary, you can have the policy discontinued or transferred to the new owner. The decedent's Estate should receive a rebate for the unused portion of the premium.

MORTGAGE INSURANCE

If the decedent had a mortgage on any parcel of real estate that he owned, he might have arranged with his lender for an insurance policy that pays off the mortgage balance in the event of his death. Look at the closing statement to see if there was a charge for mortgage insurance. Also check with the lender to determine if such a policy was purchased.

If the decedent was the sole owner of the property, then the beneficiary of that property needs to make arrangements to continue payment of the mortgage until title to the property is transferred to that beneficiary.

NOTIFY THE HOMEOWNER'S ASSOCIATION

If the decedent owned a condominium or a residence regulated by a homeowner's association, then the association will need to be notified of the death. Once the property is transferred to the proper beneficiary, he/she will need to contact the association to learn of the rules and regulations regarding ownership and to arrange to have notices of dues and assessments forwarded to the new owner.

WORK RELATED INSURANCE

If the decedent was employed, then check his records for information about work related benefits. He may have survivor benefits from a company or group life insurance plan and/or a retirement plan. Also check with the employer about company benefits. If the decedent belonged to a union, then contact them to determine whether there are any union benefits.

The decedent may have belonged to a professional, fraternal or social organization such as the local Chamber of Commerce, a Veteran's organization, the Kiwanis, AARP, the Rotary Club, etc. If he belonged to any such organization check to see whether the organization provided any type of insurance coverage.

BUSINESS OWNED BY DECEDENT

If the decedent owned his own company or was a partner in a company he may have purchased "key man" insurance. Key man insurance is a policy designed to protect the company should a valuable employee become disabled or die. Benefits are paid to the company to compensate the company for the loss of someone who is essential to the continuation of the business. Ultimately the policy benefits those who inherit the business.

If the decedent had an ownership interest in an ongoing business (sole proprietor, shareholder or partner) there may be a shareholder's or partnership agreement requiring the company to purchase the decedent's share of the business. The Personal Representative's attorney needs to investigate to see if there was a key man insurance policy and/or such purchase agreement.

If the decedent was the sole owner of a corporation and the company stock was in his name only, then it may take a Probate procedure before the company can be transferred to the new owner. If the decedent was the sole officer and Registered Agent of the company, then the Virginia State Corporation Commission needs to be notified of the identity of the new officers and Registered Agent.

The law requires each corporation to continuously maintain a Registered Agent who resides in this state. If the decedent was the Resident Agent of a corporation, then a new Agent needs to be appointed as soon as is practicable (VA 13.1-635). Forms to provide notice of the change of officers, directors and Registered Agent can be obtained by calling the State Corporation Commission:

        In state: (800) 552-7945.
        Out of state: (804) 371-9967
        Hearing impaired: TDD (804) 371-9206.

or writing to them at:

        STATE CORPORATION COMMISSION
        P.O. Box 1197
        Richmond, VA 23218

If you were not actively involved in running the business, then you might want to request a status report of the company. The report will show whether filing fees are current and will identify the officers and directors of the company.

NOTIFY ADVERTISERS

Probably the last in the world to learn of the decedent's death is the direct mail advertiser. Advertisers are nothing if not tenacious. It is not uncommon for advertisements to be mailed to the decedent for more than ten years after the death. It is not because the advertiser is trying to sell something to the decedent, but rather the people who prepare (and sell) mailing lists do not know that the person is dead.

Those who sell mailing lists may not be motivated to update the list because of the cost of doing the necessary research; and maybe even because the price of the mailing list is often based on the number of people on the list. Even those who compose their own list may decide it is less costly to mail to everyone, than take the time (and money) to update the list.

If it gives you pleasure to think of advertisers spending substantial sums for nothing, then that is what you should do (nothing). But for those of you who wince each time you see another piece of mail addressed to the decedent, you can write to the Direct Marketing Association and ask that the name be deleted from all mailing lists:

> Mail Preference Service
> Direct Marketing Association
> P.O. Box 9008
> Farmingdale, NY 11735-9008

You will need to give them the decedent's complete address, including zip code and every name variation that the decedent may have used; for example:

> Mr. Theodore James Jones
> Ted Jones   Ted J. Jones
> T. J. Jones   T. James Jones, etc.

HEALTH INSURANCE

The Health Insurance carrier probably knows of the death, but it is a good idea to contact them to determine what coverage the decedent had under that insurance plan. If you cannot find the original policy, have the insurance company send you a copy of the policy so that you can determine whether medical treatment given to the decedent before his death was covered by that policy.

 **DECEDENT ON MEDICARE**

If the decedent was covered by Medicare, you do not need to notify anyone, but you do need to know what things were covered by Medicare so that you can determine what medical bills are (or are not) covered by Medicare. The publication **MEDICARE AND YOU** explains what things are covered. The book is available in regular print (Publication HCFA 10050) and in large print (Publication HCFA 10050-LE). You can get the book by writing to the

U.S. GOVERNMENT PRINTING OFFICE
U.S. Dept. of Health and Human Services
Health Care Financing Administration
7500 Security Boulevard
Baltimore, MD 21244-1850

You can also find the publication on the Internet:

 MEDICARE WEB SITE
http:/www.medicare.gov

THE SPOUSE'S HEALTH INSURANCE

SPOUSE

If the spouse of the decedent is insured under Medicare, then the death does not affect the surviving spouse's coverage. If the spouse was not covered by Medicare but has her own health insurance that also covered the decedent, then the spouse needs to notify the employer of the death because this may affect the cost of the plan to the employer and/or the spouse.

If the spouse was covered under the decedent's policy then he/she needs to arrange for new coverage. There are state and federal laws that ensure continued coverage under the decedent's policy for a period of time depending on whether the decedent's employer falls under federal or state regulation.

If the decedent was employed by a federally regulated company (usually a company with at least twenty employees) then under the Consolidated Omnibus Budget Reconciliation Act ("COBRA") the employer must make the company health plan available to the surviving spouse and any dependent child of the decedent for at least 36 months. The employer is required to give notice to the surviving spouse that the spouse and/or dependent child have the right to continue coverage under the decedent's health plan. The spouse and/or child have 60 days from the date of death or 60 days after the employer sends notice (whichever is later) to tell the employer whether the surviving spouse and child wish to continue with the health insurance plan (29 USC 18 Sec. 1162, 1163).

The only problem with continued coverage may be the cost. Before the death, the employer may have been paying some percentage of the premium. The employer has no such duty after the death unless there was some employment agreement stating otherwise. Under COBRA, the employer may charge the spouse for the full cost of the plan plus a 2% administrative fee. If you have a question about your coverage under COBRA, you can call the U.S. Department of Labor ("DOL") at (800) 998-7542 and ask for the number of your local DOL office. You can also ask that they send you their publication **HEALTH BENEFITS UNDER COBRA**; or you can visit their Web site for more information:

 DEPARTMENT OF LABOR WEB SITE
http://www.dol.gov/dol/pwba

CONTINUED COVERAGE UNDER VIRGINIA LAW

If decedent was employed by local or state government and was covered by a health insurance plan as part of his employment (or retirement), then Virginia law requires that the family be allowed to remain covered under that plan. Coverage can continue for the decedent's minor child until the age of 21; or 25 if the child is attending college. Coverage for the surviving spouse can continue until he/she remarries.

The family member needs to contact the employer as soon as practicable after the death, if they wish to continue coverage. The cost of the policy could increase, however if the decedent was a policeman or fireman, then the cost cannot be greater than the current rate for the same class of coverage (VA 2.1-20.1:03, 2.1-20.1:04, 2.1-20.1:05).

✍ CHANGE BENEFICIARIES ✍

If the decedent was someone you named as beneficiary of your insurance policy, Will or Trust, brokerage account or pension plan, then you may need to name another beneficiary in his place:

INSURANCE POLICY ✍

If you named the decedent as the primary beneficiary of your life insurance policy, then check to see whether you named a contingent (alternate) beneficiary in the event that the decedent did not survive you. If not, you need to contact the insurance company and name a new beneficiary. If you did name a contingent beneficiary, that person is now your primary beneficiary and you need to consider whether you wish to name a new contingent beneficiary at this time.

HEALTH INSURANCE POLICY ✍

If the decedent was covered under your health insurance policy, then your employer and the health insurer need to be notified of the death because this may affect the cost of the plan to you and/or your employer.

WILL OR TRUST ✍

Most Wills provide for a contingent beneficiary in the event that the person named as beneficiary dies first. If you named the decedent as your beneficiary, then check to see whether you named an alternate beneficiary. If not, you need to have your attorney revise your Will and name a new beneficiary.

Similarly, if you are the Grantor or Settlor of a Trust and the decedent was one of the beneficiaries of your Trust, then check the Trust document to see if you named an alternate beneficiary. If not, contact your attorney to prepare an amendment to the Trust, naming a new beneficiary.

BANK AND SECURITIES ACCOUNTS ✍

If the decedent was a beneficiary of your bank or securities account, or if the decedent was a joint owner of your bank account or securities account, then it is important to contact the financial institution and tell them about the death. You may wish to arrange for a new beneficiary or joint owner at this time.

PENSION PLANS ✍

If the decedent was a beneficiary under your pension plan, then you need to notify them of his death and name a new beneficiary. Many pension plans require that you notify them within a set period of time (usually 30 days) so it is important to notify them as soon as you are able. If the decedent was a beneficiary of your Individual Retirement Account ("IRA") or of your Qualified Retirement Plan ("QRP") and you did not provide for an alternate beneficiary, then you need to name someone at this time.

Before you choose an alternate beneficiary, it is important that you understand all of the options available to you. Not an easy task. There are many complex government regulations relating to IRA and QRP accounts. And even if you believe you understood your options when you set up your account, they are scheduled to be changed beginning in 2002. You can read about the proposed regulations under 42 U.S.C 401(a)(9) in the *Federal Register* that was published on January 17, 2001, but unless you have an extensive tax background, it is just so much "legalese," i.e., incomprehensible without a professional to translate it into plain English.

Your choice of beneficiary can impact the amount of money you can withdraw each month, so it is important to consult with your accountant or tax attorney or financial planner, before you make your election.

NOTIFY CREDIT CARD COMPANIES

You need to notify the decedent's credit card companies of the death. If you can find the contract with the credit card company check to see whether the decedent had credit card insurance. If the decedent had credit card insurance, then the balance of the account is now paid in full. If you cannot find the contract contact the company and get a copy of the contract along with a statement of the balance due as of the date of death.

DESTROY DECEDENT'S CREDIT CARDS

You need to destroy all of the decedent's credit cards. If you hold a credit card jointly with the decedent, then it is important to waste no time in closing that account and opening another in your name only.

That's something Barbara knows from hard experience. She and Hank never married but they did live together for several years before he died from liver disease. Hank came from a well to do family so he had enough money to support himself and Barbara during his long illness. Hank put Barbara on all of his credit card accounts so that she could purchase things when he became too ill to go shopping with her. After the funeral, Barbara had a gathering of friends and family at their apartment. Barbara was so preoccupied with her loss that she never noticed that Hank's credit cards were missing until the bills started coming in.

Barbara did not know who ran up the bills on Hank's credit cards during the month following his death. It was obvious that Hank's signature had been forged — but who forged it? One credit card company suspected that it might have been Barbara herself, just to get out of paying for the items by saying that the card was stolen.

Because the cards were held jointly, the company held Barbara liable to either pay the debts or prove that she did not make the purchases. She was able to clear her credit record but it took several months and she had to employ an attorney to do so.

NOTIFYING OTHER CREDITORS

If a probate procedure is necessary and the decedent owed money, then it is the job of the person appointed as Personal Representative to notify the decedent's creditors of the death. The attorney who handles the probate will explain to the Personal Representative how notice is to be given.

If no probate procedure is necessary, then the next of kin can notify the creditors of the death, but before doing so, read Chapter 4: WHAT BILLS NEED TO BE PAID? That chapter explains what bills need to be paid and who is responsible to pay them.

Before any bill can be paid you need to know whether the decedent left any assets that could be used to pay those debts. The next chapter explains how to identify, and then locate all of the property owned by the decedent.

Locating the Assets 3

It is important to locate the financial records of the decedent and then carefully examine those records. Even the partner of a long-term marriage should conduct a thorough search because the surviving spouse may be unaware of all that was owned (or owed) by the decedent.

It is not unusual for a surviving spouse to be surprised when learning of the decedent's business transactions, especially in those cases where the decedent had control of family finances. One such example is that of Sam and Henrietta. They married just as soon as Sam was discharged from the army after World War II. During their marriage, Sam handled all of the finances giving Henrietta just enough money to run the household.

Every now and again Henrietta would think of getting a job. She longed to have her own source of income and some economic independence. Each time she brought up the subject Sam would loudly object. He had no patience for this new "woman's lib" thing. Sam said he got married to have a real wife — one who would cook his meals and keep house for him.

Henrietta was not the arguing type. She rationalized, saying that Sam had a delicate stomach and dust allergies. He needed her to prepare his special meals and keep an immaculate house for him. Besides, Sam had a good job with a major cruise line and he needed her to accompany him on his frequent business trips.

Once Sam retired, he was even more cautious in his spending habits. Henrietta seldom complained. She assumed the reason for his "thrift" was that they had little money and had to live on his pension.

They were married 52 years when Sam died at the age of 83. Henrietta was 81 at the time of his death. She was one very happy, very angry and very aged widow when she discovered that Sam left her with assets worth well over a million dollars!

LOCATING RECORDS

As you go through the papers of the decedent you may come across documents that indicate property ownership, such as bank registers, stock or bond certificates, insurance policies, brokerage account statements, etc. Place all evidence of ownership in a single place. You will need to contact the different companies in order to transfer title to the proper beneficiary. Chapter 5 explains how to identify the proper beneficiary of the decedent's property. Chapter 6 explains how to transfer the property to that beneficiary.

You may also need to produce evidence of the decedent's personal relationships, such as a marriage certificate, birth certificate, or naturalization papers, a Final Judgement of Divorce, military personnel records, etc. If you cannot locate his marriage certificate or birth certificate, you can get a certified copy of those records from the Vital Records office in the state where the event took place. See page 24 for Virginia's Vital Records. You can find the location and telephone number for other states by calling information or from the Internet by using your favorite search engine to locate Vital Records.

You can obtain a copy of a deceased Veteran's military record by writing to:

The National Personnel Records Center
Military Personnel Records
9700 Page Avenue
St. Louis, MO   63132-5100

They will send you form SF 180 to complete. You can get the form from the Internet at http://www.cem.va.gov
or from the National Archives and Records Administration Fax-On-Demand system. Dial (301) 713-6905 and request document number 2255.

COLLECT AND IDENTIFY KEYS

The decedent may have kept his records in a safe deposit box, so you may find that your first job is to locate the keys to the box. As you go through the personal effects of the decedent, collect and identify all the keys that you find. If you come across an unidentified key, it could be a key to a post office box (private or federal) or a safe deposit box located in a bank or in a private vault company. You will need to determine whether that key opens a box that contains property belonging to the decedent or whether the key is to a box no longer in use. Some ways to investigate are as follows:

☑   CHECK BUSINESS RECORDS

If the decedent kept receipts, look through those items to see if he paid for the rental of a post office or safe deposit box. Also, look at his check register to see if he wrote a check to the Postmaster or to any safe deposit or vault company. Look at his bank statements to see if there is any bank charge for a safe deposit box. Some banks bill separately for safe deposit boxes so check with all of the banks in which the decedent had an account to determine if he had a box with that bank.

☑   CHECK THE KEY TYPE

If you cannot identify the key, then take it to all of the local locksmiths and ask whether anyone can identify the type of facility that uses such keys. If that doesn't work, then go to each bank, post office and private safe deposit box company where the decedent shopped, worked or frequented and ask whether they use the type of key that you found.

☑   CHECK THE MAIL

Check the mail over the next several months to see if the decedent receives a statement requesting payment for the next year's rental of a post office or safe deposit box.

FORWARD THE DECEDENT'S MAIL

You may find evidence of a brokerage account, bank account, or safe deposit box by examining correspondence addressed to the decedent. If the decedent was living alone, then have the mail forwarded to the person he named as Personal Representative or Executor of his Will. If the decedent did not leave a Will then the mail should be forwarded to his next of kin. Call the Postmaster and ask him/her to send you the necessary forms to make the change. Request that the mail be forwarded for the longest period allowed by law (currently one year).

The decedent may have been renting a post office box at his local post office branch or perhaps at the branch closest to where he did his banking. Ask the Postmaster to help you determine whether the decedent was renting a post office box. If so, then you need to locate the key to the box so that you can collect the decedent's mail.

Special Situation ▷ LOST POST OFFICE BOX KEY

If the decedent had a post office box and you cannot locate the key, then contact the local postmaster and ask him/her what documentation is needed for you to gain possession of the mail in that box. As before, you will ask the Postmaster to have all future mail addressed to that box, forwarded to the Personal Representative, or if there is no Will, then to the decedent's next of kin.

WHAT TO DO WITH CHECKS

You may receive checks in the mail made out to the decedent. Social security checks, pension checks and annuity checks issued after the date of death need to be returned to the sender. (See pages 28 and 30 of this book.) Other checks need to be deposited. If a Probate procedure is necessary, then the Personal Representative will open a Probate Estate account and the checks should be deposited to that account.

If no Probate procedure is necessary, then the checks can be deposited to any account held in the name of the decedent. The decedent is not here to endorse the check, but you can deposit it to his account by writing his bank account number on the back of the check and printing beneath it "**FOR DEPOSIT ONLY.**"

The bank will accept such an endorsement and deposit the check into the decedent's account. If the check is significant in value and/or the decedent had different accounts that are accessible to different people, then there needs to be cooperation and a sense of fair play. If not, the dollar gain may not nearly offset the emotional turmoil. Such was the case with Gail. Her father made her a joint owner of his checking account to assist in paying his bills. He had macular degeneration and it was increasingly difficult for him to see. The father also had a savings account that was in his name only.

Gail's brother, Ken, had a good paying job in Alaska. Even though he lived at a distance, Ken, his wife and two children always spent the Christmas holidays with his father. Gail's good cooking added to the festivities. Each summer, their father enjoyed leaving the heat of Virginia to spend a few weeks in the cool Alaskan climate.

One July, the father purchased a round trip ticket to Alaska. It cost several hundred dollars. Just before the departure date, the father had a heart attack and died. Gail called the airline to cancel the ticket. They refunded the money in a check made out to her father. She deposited the check to the joint account.

As part of the Probate procedure, the money in the father's savings account was divided equally between Ken and his sister. Ken wondered what happened to the money from the airline tickets.

Gail explained "He paid for the tickets from the joint account, so I deposited the money back to that account. "

"Aren't you going to give me half?"

"Dad meant for me to have whatever was in that joint account. If he wanted you to have half of the money, he would have made you joint owner as well."

Ken didn't see it that way: "That refund was part of Dad's Probate Estate. It should have been deposited to his savings account to be divided equally between us. Are you going force me to argue this in court?"

Gail finally agreed to split the money with Ken, but the damage was done.

Gail complains that holidays are lonely since Dad died.

LOCATING FINANCIAL RECORDS

To locate the decedent's assets you need to find evidence of what he owned and where those assets are located. His financial records should lead you to the location of all of his assets so your first job is to locate those records. The best place to start the search is in the decedent's home. Many people keep their financial records in a single place but it is important to check the entire house to be sure you did not miss something.

CHECK THE COMPUTER

Don't overlook that computer sitting silently in the corner. It may hold the decedent's check register and all of the decedent's financial records. The computer may be programmed to protect information. If you cannot access the decedent's records, you may need to employ a computer technician or computer consultant who will be able to print out all of the information on the hard drive of the computer. You can find such a technician or consultant by looking in the telephone book under
COMPUTER SUPPORT SERVICES or
COMPUTER SYSTEM DESIGNS & CONSULTANTS.

LOCATE TITLE TO MOTOR VEHICLE

In the state of Virginia, if monies are owed on a motor vehicle (car or mobile home), the lender takes possession of the original certificate of title until the loan is paid. If you cannot find the original certificate of title, then it is either lost or monies are owed on the car and the lienholder has the original title. You can go to the Department of Motor Vehicles in the county of the decedent's residence and they will issue a replacement (duplicate) title to you. The Department of Motor Vehicles will require proof of your authority to get a copy of the Title. In some cases, they will issue the replacement title only to the Personal Representative.

It is a good idea to first call your local Department of Motor Vehicles to determine what information they require and the cost of obtaining the replacement Title (currently $5). The toll free number for the Department of Motor Vehicles is (866) 368-5463. For the hearing impaired call (800) 272-9268 (TDD).

Once you get the Title Certificate, you may find that there is a lien on the car. If so, you need to contact the lienholder and get a copy of the contract that is the basis of the loan

 **THE LEASED CAR**

You may find that the car is leased and not owned by the decedent. If so, contact the lessor and get a copy of the lease agreement. Check to see whether the decedent had life insurance as part of the agreement. If he did, then the lease may now be paid in full and the beneficiary of the car should be able to use the car for the remainder of the leasing period, or take title to the car, whichever option is available under the lease agreement. The Personal Representative (or the beneficiary) can send the death certificate to the leasing company with a copy of the contract and a letter requesting that the transfer be made.

If the lease is not paid in full upon the decedent's death, then arrangements need to be made to satisfy the terms of the agreement. See Chapter 6 for information about transferring a leased car.

LOCATE CONTRACTS

If the decedent belonged to a health club or gym, he may have prepaid for the year. Look for the club contract. It will give the terms of the agreement. If you cannot locate the contract then contact the company for a copy of the agreement. If the contract was prepaid, then determine whether the agreement provides for a refund for the unused portion.

SERVICE CONTRACT

Many people purchase appliance service contracts to have their appliances serviced in the event that an appliance should need repair. If the decedent had a security system then he may have had a service contract with a company to monitor the system and contact the police in the event of a break-in.

If the decedent had a service contract, then you need to locate it and determine whether it can be assigned to the new owner of the property. If the contract is assignable, the new owner can reimburse the decedent's Estate for the unused portion. If the contract cannot be assigned, then once the property is transferred, try to obtain a refund for the unused portion of the contract.

Special Situation

DECEDENT'S RESIDENTIAL LEASE

If the decedent was renting his residence, then he may have a written lease agreement. It is important to locate the lease because the decedent's Estate may be responsible for payments under the lease. If you cannot locate the lease, then ask the landlord for a copy. If the landlord reports that there was no written lease, then verify that the decedent was on a month to month basis and then work out a mutually agreeable time in which to vacate the premises.

If a written lease is in effect, then determine the end of the lease period, and whether there was a security deposit. Ask whether the landlord will agree to cancel the lease on the condition that the property is left in good condition. If the landlord says that the Estate is responsible to pay the balance of the lease, then it is prudent to have an attorney review the lease to determine what rights and responsibilities remain now that the tenant is deceased.

☎ **LAWYER**

DECEDENT'S ONGOING BUSINESS

If the decedent was the sole owner of a business, or if he owned a partnership interest in a business, the Personal Representative needs to contact the company accountant to obtain the company's business records. If there is a company attorney, then the attorney may be able to assist in obtaining the records. If you are a beneficiary of the Estate, consider consulting with your own attorney to determine what rights and responsibilities you may have in the business.

COLLECT TAX RECORDS

The decedent's final state and federal income tax returns need to be filed so you should locate all of his tax records for the past 3 years. If you cannot locate his prior tax records, then check his personal telephone book and/or his personal bank register to see if he employed someone to prepare his taxes. If you can locate his tax preparer, then he/she should have a copy of those records.

If you are unable to locate the decedent's federal tax returns then they can be obtained from the IRS. The IRS will send copies of the decedent's tax filings to anyone who has a **fiduciary relationship** with the decedent. The IRS considers the following people to be a fiduciary:

➢ the person appointed as the Personal Representative of the decedent's Estate

➢ the Successor Trustee of the decedent's trust

➢ if the person died without a Will, then whoever is legally entitled to possession of the decedent's property (See Chapter 5 for the Laws of Descent).

The fiduciary can receive copies of the decedent's tax filings by notifying IRS that he/she is acting in a fiduciary capacity, and then requesting the copies.

To notify the IRS of the fiduciary capacity file Form 56:
NOTICE CONCERNING FIDUCIARY RELATIONSHIP

To request the copies, file IRS Form 4506:
REQUEST FOR COPY OR TRANSCRIPT OF TAX FORM
Your accountant can file these forms for you or you can obtain the forms from the IRS by calling (800) 829-3676 or you can download them from the Internet:

IRS FORMS WEB SITE
http://www.irs.gov/forms_pubs/forms.html

LOCATE STATE INCOME TAX RETURN

If you cannot locate the decedent's state income tax return you can get a copy from the Virginia Department of Taxation. If a Probate procedure is necessary, then the Personal Representative can get the copy. If no Probate is necessary, and you are next of kin, then you can request a copy by writing to:

VIRGINIA DEPARTMENT OF TAXATION
CUSTOMER SERVICE
P.O. Box 1115
Richmond, VA   23218

Before writing, you may want to call the Department (804) 367-2062 and ask what information or document they require in order for you to obtain a copy of the return.

LOCATE OUT OF STATE ACCOUNTS

If the decedent had out of state bank or brokerage accounts, then you might be able to locate them if they mail the decedent monthly or quarterly statements. Not all institutions do so, but all institutions are required to send out an IRS tax form 1099 each year giving the amount of interest earned on that account. Once the forms come in, you will learn the location of all of the decedent's active accounts.

COLLECT DEEDS

Collect the deeds to all property owned by the decedent. Many people keep deeds in a safe deposit box. If you cannot find the deed in the decedent's home, then you need to determine whether he had a safe deposit box; and if so, you will need to examine the contents of the box. Access to the safe deposit box is discussed at the end of this chapter.

If you know that the decedent owned real property (lot, residence, condominium, cooperative, time share, etc.) but you cannot locate the deed, then contact the Clerk of the Circuit Court in the county where the property is located. The Clerk of Courts can provide you with a certified copy of the last recorded deed.

You will need to identify the parcel of land by giving the Clerk the legal description of the land or its tax map identification number. You can find this information on the last tax bill sent to the decedent. If you cannot find the last property tax bill, then call the property appraiser or the tax collector's office and they will give you the information.

You can use the same procedure if you cannot locate the deed to property owned by the decedent in another state, namely, check with the recording department in the county where the property is located. In some states the County Recorder or Registrar of Deeds is in charge of the recording department.

 **LAWYER**

OUT OF STATE PROPERTY OR RESIDENCE

If the decedent had his residence in Virginia and owned property in another state, then you may need to have an initial Probate procedure in Virginia and an *ancillary* (secondary) Probate procedure in the other state. If the decedent had his residence in another state and owned property in Virginia, then it may need to be done the other way around; namely, you may need to conduct the initial Probate in the other state and the ancillary Probate in Virginia (VA 64.1-92).

Some states have laws that determine the location of the initial administration, so it may be that you have no choice in the matter. In many states, however, the choice of state is up to the Personal Representative. Before depositing the Will with the court, you need to determine whether you have a choice in the matter; and if so, then you need to make an informed decision as to the best place for the initial Probate procedure.

To make that determination you need to consult with an attorney in each state who is experienced in Probate matters. Convenience is an important consideration, but you also need to consider that each state has its own tax structure and Probate statutes. Ask each attorney whether the location of the initial Probate procedure will have any effect on the total cost of the Probate procedure, who is to inherit the property or how much the Estate will be taxed.

FINDING LOST OR ABANDONED PROPERTY

If the decedent was forgetful, he may have money in a lost bank account or abandoned safe deposit box. Property that is unclaimed is turned over the to the Virginia Department of Treasury after a period of time as set by Virginia law. The time period depends on the item:.

- ⌛ 1 year for unclaimed wages
- ⌛ 1 year after service is discontinued for an unclaimed utility deposit
- ⌛ 5 years after the lease expires for items contained in a safe deposit box
- ⌛ 7 years for an unclaimed money order
- ⌛ 15 years from the date of issue of a travelers check

Before turning the property over to the state, the holder of the unclaimed property must make a good faith effort to contact the owner and return the property to the owner. Once the property is turned over to the Department of Treasury, the Commissioner will publish a notice entitled "Commonwealth of Virginia Unclaimed Property List" in a newspaper of general circulation in the area of the last known address of the owner of the property.

If a tangible item (such as jewelry) remains unclaimed, the Commissioner will convert it to cash by holding a public auction. The proceeds of the sale are placed in the state Literary Fund. The Literary Fund is used to finance school construction. There is no time limit on claiming funds. If the item is later claimed, the Commissioner will give the proceeds of the sale to the owner (or his heir), plus interest for the period the money was held in the Literary Fund (VA 55-210.3:02, 55-210.3:3, 55-210.5, 55-210.8:2, 55-210.12, 55-210.13, 55.210.21).

You can determine whether there is a record identifying the decedent as the owner of abandoned property in Virginia by writing to:

VIRGINIA DEPARTMENT OF TREASURY
Division of Unclaimed Property
P.O. Box 2478
Richmond, VA 23218

or by calling them at (800) 468-1088.

CLAIMS IN OTHER STATES

Each state has an agency or department that is responsible for handling lost, abandoned or unclaimed property located within that state. If the decedent had residences in other states, then call the UNCLAIMED or ABANDONED PROPERTY department of the state Treasury to see if the decedent has unclaimed property in that state. Many states (including Virginia) have information about unclaimed property for that state on the Internet:

 UNCLAIMED PROPERTY WEB SITE
http://www.missingmoney.com

CLAIMS FOR DECEDENT VICTIMS OF HOLOCAUST

The New York State Banking Department has a special Claims Processing Office for Holocaust survivors or their heirs. The office processes claims for Swiss bank accounts that were dormant since the end of World War II. If the decedent was a victim of the Holocaust, you can get information about money that may be due to the decedent's Estate by calling (800) 695-3318.

CLAIMS FOR IRS TAX REFUNDS

The IRS reports that some 90,000 tax refund checks representing 67.4 million dollars were returned to them as being not deliverable. They keep the information on file and will forward the full amount once they locate the taxpayer. You can determine whether they are holding a check for the decedent by calling the IRS at (800) 829-1040.

FILING AND RECORDING THE WILL

The decedent's original Will needs to be filed with the Clerk in the county of his residence. If the decedent owned property in Virginia, but did not live here, then the Will needs to be deposited with the Clerk in the county where the property is located (VA 64.1-75).

The Clerk will accept an original Will only and not a copy, so it is important to hand carry the original document to the Clerk. If you are the Executor of the Will, you can give it to your attorney to file with the court as part of the Probate procedure. Make a copy of the Will for your own records before delivering it to the Clerk or to your attorney.

A Will is valid in Virginia if it was signed by the decedent in the presence of two competent witnesses, and the witnesses also signed the Will (VA 64.1-49). If the Will was signed by a Notary Public verifying the identity of the Will maker and the two witnesses, then it is considered to be *self-proved.* If the Will is not self-proved, then the Clerk will require testimony from the witnesses to prove that the Will is valid.

Once the Will has been accepted into Probate, the Clerk will record it and index it in the General Index of Wills. If the decedent owned real property in Virginia, the Personal Representative needs to have a copy of the Will recorded in the county where the property is located. Once the Will is recorded, anyone who examines title to the property will know that the owner is now deceased and who inherited his property (VA 64.1-94).

WILL DRAFTED IN ANOTHER STATE OR COUNTRY

If the Will was drafted in another state or country and it conforms to Virginia law, then the Clerk will accept that Will into Probate here in Virginia.

If the decedent was a resident of another state or country, and had a Will that was valid there, but not in Virginia, the Clerk will allow the Will to be Probated here in Virginia, provided there is no real property involved. If real property is involved, then the Will must be admitted into Probate in the state or country where it is valid. Once the Will is certified as being valid elsewhere, the Clerk will accept an authenticated copy of the Will into Probate here in Virginia (VA 64.1-53, 64.1-92).

THE INTERNATIONAL WILL
Virginia has adopted the Uniform International Wills Act. One of the requirements of the Act, is to have a certificate attached to the Will that verifies the identity of the person making the Will and the identity of two witnesses to the Will. The certificate must be signed by someone authorized to do so, such as an attorney or someone in the diplomatic service of the United States.

A Will that complies with these requirements is essentially self-proved and will be admitted into Probate in Virginia without any further proof of its validity. If the Will is written in a foreign language, then it must be translated into English before it can be admitted into Probate (VA 64.1-96.2, 64.1-96.3, 64.1-96.6, 64.1-96.10).

THE MISSING WILL

People tend to put off making a Will until they think they need to. For many, that need arises when they are elderly and/or seriously ill and have assets that they want to leave to someone. Young people with few assets usually do not have a Will. People who are aged and with significant assets usually have a Will or Trust. A survey conducted for the American Association of Retired Persons ("AARP") found that the probability of having a Will increases with age. Forty-four percent of those surveyed who were between the ages of 50 to 54 had a Will. This increased to 85% for those who were 80 and older. You can find more details of the survey at their Web site:

 AARP WEB SITE
http://research.aarp.org

Those who make a Will, usually tell the person that they appoint as Executor, of the existence of the Will. Chances are, that someone in the decedent's circle of family and friends, knows whether there is a Will. If you believe that the decedent had a Will, but you cannot find it, then there are at least three places to check out:

⇨ THE DECEDENT'S ATTORNEY
Look at the decedent's checkbook for the past few years and see whether he paid any attorney fees. If you are able to locate the decedent's attorney, then call and inquire whether the attorney ever drafted a Will for the decedent, and if so, whether the attorney has the original Will in his possession. If the attorney has the original Will, then ask the attorney to forward the Will to the Clerk. Asking the attorney to forward the Will to the court does not obligate you to employ the attorney should you later find that a Probate procedure is necessary.

⇨ THE CLERK OF THE CIRCUIT COURT

Virginia law gives residents the right to deposit their Will with the Clerk of the Circuit Court. Check with the Clerk in any city or county where the decedent lived. If the Will is on file, the Clerk will deliver the Will to the Executor of the Will. If you are the Executor, then go to the Court and give the Clerk proof of your identity and a certified copy of the death certificate (VA 64.1-56).

⇨ THE SAFE DEPOSIT BOX

Most people keep their original Will in a safe deposit box. If you believe that the decedent had a Will but you cannot find it, then check to see if the decedent had a safe deposit box. If he did, you will need to gain entry to that box to see whether the Will is in the box. See page 74 for an explanation of how to gain entry to the safe deposit box.

 **LAWYER**   A COPY BUT NO ORIGINAL

In Virginia, a person can revoke his Will simply by destroying it. If you have a copy of the Will and cannot find the original, the Clerk will presume that the decedent revoked that Will. You can *petition* (ask) the Court to accept the copy into Probate, but you will need to prove that the document is a true copy of the decedent's valid Will. You will also need to prove that the decedent had no intention of revoking that Will. These are not easy things to prove. It make take a trial by jury to prove the Will (VA 64.1-83, 64.1-88)

If you want to have a copy of the Will admitted into Probate, you will need to employ an attorney experienced in Probate matters to present your case to the Court.

ACCESSING THE SAFE DEPOSIT BOX

If the decedent rented a safe deposit box with another person, each with free access to the box, then once the surviving joint renter of the box can go to the box and remove the contents of the box (VA 6.1-332). If the decedent had a safe deposit in his name alone and you think his Will may be in the safe deposit box, you can ask the Lessor of the box (usually a bank) to let you inspect the box to see if the Will is there. Under Virginia law, the Lessor may allow a spouse or next of kin to look at the contents of the box under the supervision of an officer or employee of the company. If the Will is there, you or the Lessor can arrange to have it delivered to the Clerk of the Circuit Court. You may save yourself time and hassle, if you first call the financial institution and make an appointment to meet with an officer. Ask what identification they will require of you. Most will want to see the death certificate. They may also want to see your driver's license as proof that you are the spouse or next of kin.

Other than the Will, nothing else can be removed from the safe deposit box without authorization from the Clerk of the Circuit Court (VA 6.1-332.1). Whether or not the Will is in the box, it is a good idea to take an inventory of the items contained within the box. If there needs to be a Probate procedure, then the Personal Representative can gain access to the safe deposit box as soon as he obtains his Letters.

Once you have located all of the decedent's property you may think the next step is to determine who gets to inherit that property. But some of that property may be needed to pay monies owed by the decedent; so the next step is to determine what, if any, bills need to be paid. And that is the topic of the next chapter.

What Bills Need To Be Paid? 4

Virginia is a state that respects the rights of creditors. If the Estate of the decedent has sufficient assets, then the Personal Representative of the decedent's Estate has the duty to be sure that all valid ***claims against the Estate*** (demands for payment) are paid. If the decedent had debts, but no money or property, then of course, there is no way to pay the bills. The only remaining question is whether anyone else is responsible to pay those bills. If the decedent was married, then the first person the creditor will look to, is the decedent's spouse. To understand the basis of this expectation, you need to know a bit of the history of our legal system.

Our laws are derived from the English Common Law. Under early English Common law, a single woman had the right to own property in her own name and also the right to contract to buy or sell property. When a woman married, her legal identity merged with her spouse. She could not hold property free from her husband's claim or control. She could no longer enter into a contract without her husband's permission.

Once married, a woman became financially dependent on her husband. He, in turn, became legally responsible to provide his wife with basic necessities — food, clothing, shelter and medical services. If anyone provided basic necessities to his wife, then, regardless of whether the husband agreed to be responsible for the debt, he became obliged to pay for them. This law was called the DOCTRINE OF NECESSARIES.

In the United States, a series of Married Women's Rights Acts were passed giving a married woman the right to own property. Married woman have had the right to own property in Virginia since April 4, 1877 (VA 55-35).

After these laws were passed, cases followed that tested whether the Doctrine of Necessaries still applied. Judges had to decide:

If a wife can own property and contract to pay for her own necessaries, should her husband be responsible for her debts, in the event that she does not have enough money to pay for them?

For those states deciding to continue to hold the husband liable, a second question to be decided was:

If the husband is responsible for his wife's necessaries, should she be responsible for his?

In some states, notably Florida, courts decided that neither partner was responsible to pay the other's necessities, unless they contracted or agreed to do so. In Virginia, the Supreme Court refused to rule on the issue saying that it was something the legislature needed to decide (*Schilling v. Bedford Co. Hospital*, 225 Va. 539 (1983), 303 S.E.2d 905).

The Virginia legislature responded to the invitation and expanded the Doctrine so that each partner is responsible to pay for necessaries. If the spouse who made the contract or purchase, does not have sufficient funds to pay for necessaries, then his/her spouse is equally liable for the debt. The non-contracting spouse is not liable for the necessaries if the couple is permanently separated. Other than for necessaries, neither spouse is responsible to pay for the other's debts unless they both agreed to be liable (VA 55-37).

JOINT DEBTS

A *joint debt* is a debt that two or more people are responsible to pay. Usually the contract or promissory note reads that the parties agree to *joint and several liability*, meaning they all agree to pay the debt and each of them promises to be personally responsible to pay the debt. A joint debt can also be in the form of monies owed by one person with payment guaranteed by another person. If the person who owes the money does not pay, then the *guarantor* (the person who guaranteed payment) is responsible to make payment.

Hospital bills, nursing home bills, funeral expenses, legal fees incurred because of the decedent's death are all debts of the decedent's Estate. They are not joint debts unless someone guaranteed payment for the monies owed. Hospital and nursing home bills are considered to be necessaries, so if the decedent was married and there are not sufficient funds in the Estate to pay for these bills, the spouse is responsible for payment, regardless of whether the spouse agreed to be jointly liable for the debt.

OTHER JOINT SPOUSAL DEBTS

The surviving spouse is responsible to pay for loans signed by the spouse and decedent. For example, if they both were authorized to use a credit card, and there is no money in the decedent's Estate, then the surviving spouse must pay the debt. Property taxes are a joint debt if the decedent and the spouse both owned the property.

JOINT PROPERTY BUT NO JOINT DEBT

Suppose all of the decedent's funds are held jointly with a family member and the joint owner of the bank account did not agree to pay those debts. Can the creditor require that half of the joint funds be set aside to pay the debt? In Virginia, the answer is "yes," but with some restrictions. The Personal Representative is under no duty to ask for the monies in the joint account, but if someone writes to the Personal Representative asking that those monies be used to pay a debt, then the Personal Representative will ask the financial institution to freeze the account and not distribute the monies until the matter is settled by the Probate Court. The written demand must be made within 6 months from the date the Personal Representative is appointed, so if that demand is not made within that time, whoever is entitled to the decedent's share of the account is free to keep it (VA 64.1-140).

BUT NOT EXEMPT FROM UNCLE SAM

The surviving joint owner of an account has no obligation to use the joint account funds to pay the decedent's creditors unless a claim is made on the account within 6 months. However, the decedent's share of the joint account is part of his **Taxable** Estate. If federal or state taxes are due, whoever takes the decedent's share of the joint account may be required to pay whatever taxes are due on the decedent's share of that account — unless the decedent made some other provision for the payment of taxes. For example, if the decedent gave instructions in his Will that all his taxes are to be paid from monies set aside for that purpose, then the Personal Representative will follow those directions (VA 64.1-160, 64.1-161, 64.1-165).

NO MONEY — NO PROPERTY

If the decedent owed money then the debt needs to be paid from assets owned by the decedent — which leads to the next question "Did the decedent have any money in his own name when he died?"

If the decedent died without any money or property in his name, then there is no money to pay any creditor. The only question that remains is whether anyone else is liable to pay those bills. The issue of payment most often arises in relation to services provided by nursing homes. When a person enters a nursing home, he is usually too ill to speak for himself or even sign his name. In such cases, the nursing home administrator will ask the spouse or a family member to sign a battery of papers on behalf of the patient before allowing the patient to enter the facility. Buried in that battery of papers may be a statement that the family member agrees to be responsible for payment to the nursing home. If the family member refuses to guarantee payment and the patient's finances are limited, then the facility may refuse to admit the patient.

If a nursing home accepts Medicare or Medicaid payments, then, under the Federal Nursing Home Reform Law, the nursing home is prohibited from requiring a family member to guarantee payment as a condition of allowing the patient to enter that facility (USC Title 42 §1395I-3(c)(5)(A)(ii)). Nonetheless, it is common practice for a nursing home, in effect, to say "Either someone agrees to pay for the patient's bill or you need to find a different facility."

Their position is understandable. Most nursing homes are business establishments and not charitable organizations. The nursing home must be paid for the services they provide or they soon will be out of business. For an insolvent patient, the solution to the problem is to have the patient admitted to a facility as a Medicaid patient.

But what if the decedent had some money when he entered the nursing home and you agreed to guarantee payment to the nursing home?

What if you feel that you were coerced into signing as a guarantor?

Are you now liable to pay the decedent's final nursing home bill if your family member died without funds?

An experienced Elder Law attorney will be able to answer these questions after examining the documents that you signed and the conditions under which the patient entered the nursing home.

PAYING THE DECEDENT'S BILLS

If the decedent was married and no Probate procedure is necessary, then the surviving spouse needs to make provision for paying bills they were both responsible to pay. If the decedent was not married and he owned property belonging to him alone, such as a bank account, securities or real property, then paying monies owed by the decedent falls to the Personal Representative.

Once the Probate procedure begins, all of the decedent's creditors will be given an opportunity to come forward and produce evidence showing how much is owed. The Personal Representative needs to look over each unpaid invoice and decide whether it is a valid bill. The problem with making that decision is that the decedent is not here to say whether he actually received the goods and services now being billed to his Estate.

That is especially the case for medical or nursing care bills. An example of improper billing brought to the attention of this author was that of a bill submitted for a physical examination of the decedent. The bill listed the date of the examination as July 10th, but the decedent died on July 9th. Other incorrect billings may not be as obvious, so each invoice needs to be carefully examined.

If the Personal Representative decides to challenge a bill, and is unable to settle the matter with the creditor, then the Probate court will decide whether the debt is valid and should be paid.

MEDICAL BILLS COVERED BY INSURANCE

If the decedent had health insurance you may receive an invoice stamped "THIS IS NOT A BILL." This means the health care provider has submitted the bill to the decedent's health insurance company and expects to be paid by them. Even though payment is not requested, it is important to verify that the bill is valid for two reasons:

➤ **LATER LIABILITY**

If the insurer refuses to pay the claim, the facility will seek payment from whoever is in possession of the decedent's property, and that may reduce the amount inherited by the beneficiaries.

➤ **INCREASED HEALTH CARE COSTS**

Regardless of whether the decedent was covered by a private health care insurer or Medicare, improper billing increases the cost of health insurance to all of us. Consumers pay high premiums for health coverage. We, as taxpayers, all share the cost of Medicare. If unnecessary or fraudulent billing is not checked, then ultimately, we all pay.

Special Situation MEDICARE FRAUD

If you believe that you have come across a case of Medicare fraud, you can call the ANTI-FRAUD HOTLINE (800)447-8477 and report the incident to the Office of the Inspector General of the United States Department of Health and Human Services.

HOW TO CHECK MEDICARE BILLING

If the decedent was covered by Medicare, then an important billing question is whether the health care provider agreed to accept Medicare *assignment of benefits*, meaning that they agreed to accept payment directly from Medicare. If so, the maximum liability for the patient is **20%** of the amount determined as reasonable by Medicare. For example, suppose a doctor bills Medicare $1,000 for medical treatment of the decedent. If Medicare determines that a reasonable fee is $800, then the patient is liable for 20% of the $800 ($160).

Health care providers who do not accept Medicare assignment bill the patient directly. They can charge up to 15% more than the amount allowed by Medicare. If the decedent knew and agreed to be liable for the payment, then his Estate may be liable for whatever Medicare doesn't pay. For example, if a doctor's bill is $1,000 and Medicare allows $800, then Medicare will reimburse the decedent's Estate 80% of $800 ($640). The doctor may charge the Estate 15% more than the $800 ($920) and the Estate may be liable for the difference: $920 - $640 or $280.

To summarize:
For health care providers accepting Medicare assignment, the most they can bill the decedent's Estate is 20% of what Medicare allows (not 20% of what they bill.)

Those who do not accept Medicare assignment, can bill 15% more than the amount allowed by Medicare. The decedent's Estate may be liable for the difference between the amount billed and the amount paid by Medicare.

In either case, if the decedent had secondary health care insurance, then the secondary insurer may be responsible to pay for the difference.

DENIAL OF MEDICARE COVERAGE

If the health care provider reports to you that service provided to the decedent are not covered by Medicare, or if the facility submits the bill to Medicare and Medicare refuses to pay, then check to see if you agree with that ruling by determining what services are covered under Medicare. See page 45 of this book for information about how to obtain a pamphlet that explains what medical treatments are covered under Medicare.

If you have specific billing questions about Part A, you can call United Government Services at (540) 985-3931. For the hearing impaired call (540) 767-7103 TTY. For Part B questions call Trailblazer Health Enterprises (800) 444-4606.

APPEALING THE DECISION

If you believe that the decedent was wrongly denied coverage, then you can appeal that decision. The State Health Insurance Assistance Program ("SHIP") can explain how to go about filing a Medicare appeal. You can call them at (800) 552-3402. If want a local attorney to assist with your appeal, call the Virginia Bar for a referral to an attorney experienced in Medicare appeals. Some attorneys work pro bono (literally for the public good; i.e. without charge) but most charge to assist in an appeal. Federal statute 42 U.S.C. §406(a)(2)(A) limits the amount an attorney may charge for a successful Medicare appeal to 25% of the amount recovered or $4,000, whichever is the smaller amount.

DECEDENT ON MEDICAID

Medicaid is a program that provides medical and long term nursing care for people with low income and limited resources. The program is funded jointly by the federal and state government. Federal law requires the state to recover monies spent from the Estate of a Medicaid recipient who was 55 or older when the decedent received Medicaid assistance. The state will seek reimbursement for the cost of nursing home care or for home based care or for other community based services. Federal law prohibits any recovery of monies spent, until the surviving spouse, and/or disabled child of the decedent are deceased (42 U.S.C. 1396(p)).

Even if the Medicaid recipient is single, there usually is no money to recover because to qualify for Medicaid in Virginia, a person may not have more than $3,500 in assets (VA 32.1-325). Sometimes it happens that a person on Medicaid dies and his Estate later receives money perhaps as part of a settlement of a lawsuit. In such case, a Probate procedure will be necessary. The Personal Representative needs to send notice to the Department of Medical Assistance Services and give them an opportunity to file a claim against the Estate for monies spent by the state on behalf of the decedent (VA 32.1-326.1).

SOME THINGS ARE CREDITOR PROOF

Sometimes it happens that the decedent had money or property titled in his name only, but he also had a significant amount of debt. In such cases the beneficiaries may wonder whether they should go through a Probate procedure if there will be little, if anything, left after the creditors are paid. Before making the decision consider that some assets are protected under Virginia law:

✧ LIFE INSURANCE PROCEEDS ✧

The beneficiary of a life insurance policy takes the proceeds free of monies owed by the decedent, and this is so regardless of the value of the insurance policy. The only exception is the purchase of a policy to defraud creditors. For example, suppose the decedent owed a large sum of money and instead of paying the debt, he used that sum to purchase a life insurance policy. If the creditor can prove that the purpose of the purchase was to avoid paying the debt, then the money paid by the decedent for the policy, plus interest on that money, must be paid to the creditors from the proceeds of the policy (VA 38.2-3122).

✧ PREPAID TUITION ✧

Prepaid tuition contracts in the state of Virginia are creditor proof. If the decedent was contributing to the contract for the benefit of another, then the beneficiary is entitled to the proceeds of the contract free of the claims of the creditors of the decedent. Similarly, if the decedent was the named beneficiary of a prepaid tuition contract, then those funds are not available to pay any of his debts (VA 23-38.81).

✧ PENSION PLANS ✧

Annuities, pensions, profit sharing or other retirement plans regulated by the federal Employee Retirement Income Security Act of 1974 ("ERISA"), including IRA accounts and plans identified by the Internal Revenue Code as 401 and 403(a & b), 408, 408A, 409 (as in effect prior to its repeal) and 457 are creditor proof. Monies received by a beneficiary of such plans are protected from the decedent's creditors with some qualifications:

EXEMPTION LIMITED TO $17,500 PER YEAR

There is a limit on the amount of the monies that are exempt from creditors. The amount exempted can be no greater than is necessary to pay the beneficiary $17,500 per year for life. The amount exempted depends on the life expectancy of the beneficiary at the time the exemption is claimed. For example, if the beneficiary is 60 years old then up to $89,512.50 is protected from the decedent's creditors. Virginia statute 34-34 has an actuary table that you can use to figure out how much of the decedent's pension is protected. You will have no trouble using the table if you are very, very, good at math. The rest of us will need the assistance of accountant or an attorney.

NO EXEMPTION FOR TAXES

In general, income taxes are not paid when money is placed in a retirement plan. Taxes are paid when the monies are withdrawn from the account regardless of whether the monies are withdrawn by the retiree or the person he named as beneficiary of the retirement plan. If you are inheriting money from the decedent's pension, annuity or retirement allowance, then you may need to pay taxes on those monies. You should to consult with an accountant or an attorney to determine how much money needs to be set aside to pay for federal and state income taxes.

If the decedent was a resident of the state of Virginia, then his surviving spouse and minor children have certain rights that must be satisfied before any of the decedent's creditors can be paid:

FAMILY ALLOWANCE

The spouse and minor children whom the decedent was obliged to support, are entitled to receive money for their maintenance while Probate is being conducted. This maintenance is called a *Family Allowance*. The allowance can be paid in periodic installments up to $1,000 per month, or in a single lump sum, up to $12,000 per year. The money is paid to the surviving spouse, but if the minor child does not live with the spouse, then the allowance is paid to the child's custodian. The Family Allowance cannot be paid for more than a year if there is not enough money in the Estate to pay for all of the valid claims against the decedent's Estate.

The Family Allowance is given in addition to any benefit that the spouse or child may receive from the decedent's Estate. If the spouse or child dies before receiving their allowance, then the right of that person to receive the payment terminates (VA 64.1-151.1, 64.1-151.4).

EXEMPT PROPERTY

In addition to the Family Allowance, the surviving spouse may keep the decedent's household furniture, personal effects, furnishings, appliances, and automobiles, up to a total value of $10,000, not including monies owed on any of the items. If there is no surviving spouse, then the decedent's minor child is entitled to keep this *Exempt Property*. If the decedent left more than one minor child, then they will share the Exempt Property, equally (VA 64.1-151.2).

✧ THE HOMESTEAD ALLOWANCE ✧

In addition to the Family Allowance and Exempt Property, the surviving spouse is entitled to a *Homestead Allowance* in the amount of $10,000. If there is no surviving spouse, then the decedent's minor children are entitled to the Homestead Allowance which they will share equally between them. The Homestead Allowance is paid after the Family Allowance is paid and the Exempt Property distributed.

The Homestead Allowance has priority over any creditor, but if the spouse or child decides to take the Homestead Allowance, then they will not be able to inherit anything else from the decedent's Estate. If there is not enough money in the Estate to pay all of the decedent's debts, then the spouse (or child) will at least inherit the $10,000. If there are sufficient monies available to pay all debts, then the spouse or child will probably do better to not take their Homestead Allowance, but rather take their share of the inheritance (VA 64.1-151.3).

✧ THERE IS A PRIORITY OF PAYMENT ✧

Next to consider is that not all Probate debts are equal. Virginia Statute establishes an order of priority for payment of claims made against the decedent's Estate:

CLASS 1:   COST OF ADMINISTRATION
Top priority to costs associated with the administration of the Estate. This includes filing fees, attorney fees, Personal Representative fees, accounting and appraisal fees, etc..

CLASS 2: FAMILY ALLOWANCE, EXEMPT PROPERTY
AND HOMESTEAD ALLOWANCE
If the decedent was survived by a spouse and/or minor child, then they are entitled to a Family Allowance for their maintenance during the Probate procedure. The spouse is entitled to keep the decedent's personal property (up to $10,000 in value) exempt from the claims of creditors. The spouse is entitled to keep another $10,000 as a Homestead Allowance (see previous page for details).

CLASS 3: FUNERAL EXPENSES
Anyone who paid for the decedent's funeral is entitled to be reimbursed. Up to $2,000 of that expense is a Class 3 debt. Anything over that value becomes a Class 8 claim.

CLASS 4:   FEDERAL TAXES
Federal taxes that are entitled to priority under federal law are a Class 4 debt.

CLASS 5: MEDICAL AND HOSPITAL EXPENSES
Fifth in line are the medical and hospital expenses of the decedent's last illness. People who provided care to the decedent prior to death are entitled to compensation. People who provided goods or services are entitled to $150 as a Class 5 debt. Each hospital or nursing home is entitled to $400 for care given. Monies owed that are over these values become a Class 8 claim.

CLASS 6: COMMONWEALTH TAXES

Debts and taxes owed to the Commonwealth of Virginia are a Class 6 debt.

CLASS 7: FIDUCIARY FUNDS

If the decedent was serving as a fiduciary (Guardian, Conservator, Personal Representative for someone else's Estate, etc.) and the decedent held money for the credit of another, then those funds become a Class 7 debt, regardless of whether there was a bond to ensure that the decedent performed his duties.

CLASS 8: ALL OTHER CLAIMS

There is no preference of payment within a given class. If there is not sufficient money to pay everyone in a given class, then whatever money is available is prorated among them. Creditors must file their claim no later than one year after the Personal Representative is appointed, otherwise they lose any priority that they may have (VA 64.1-157, 64.1-158).

DISPUTED CLAIMS

The Judge of each Circuit Court appoints someone (usually an attorney) to be **Commissioner of Accounts**. It is the job of the Commissioner to supervise those who have been appointed as a fiduciary in that Circuit. If there is a disagreement about paying a debt, then any interested party (Personal Representative, creditor, beneficiary) can ask for a hearing before the Commissioner. Within 60 days of the hearing, the Commissioner will decide the matter. If anyone disagrees with his decision, they can file an exception with the Judge. The Judge will examine the evidence and may hold a hearing or a trial before he rules on the matter (VA 26-8, 26-32, 26-33, 64.1-171, 64.1-172).

There are federal and state laws that set time periods for pursuing a claim. Anyone who wishes to take court action must do so within the time set by the given Statute of Limitation. For example, in Virginia, the Statute of Limitation for bringing suit against a doctor for malpractice is two years from the date of injury. If the decedent promised to pay a debt and defaulted, then there lender has three years to sue to collect the debt. If the debt was in writing, then the lender has 5 years to sue for monies due and owing under a promissory note, etc. (VA 8.01-243, 8.01-243.1, 8.01-246).

These time periods can be extended under certain circumstances, but in general, if the person does not sue within the period set by the Statute of Limitations, they lose the right to pursue the claim.

If someone files a claim against the Estate and the Statute of Limitation for that claim has passed, then the Personal Representative is under no duty to pay that claim.

 **LAWYER**

DECEDENT LEAVING CONSIDERABLE DEBT

If the decedent died leaving much debt and no property, then the solution is simple. No Probate, no one gets paid. But if the decedent had property and died owing more money than the property was worth, his heirs may decide that going through a Probate procedure is just not worth the effort.

This may not be the best decision. Some creditors are tenacious and will use whatever legal strategy is available in order to be paid, including initiating the Probate procedure themselves. If no one starts a Probate procedure, then 30 days from the date of death, a creditor can petition the court to be appointed as Personal Representative of the Estate. (VA 64.1-116).

Family members may object to having a creditor as a Personal Representative, so there could be a court battle over who has priority to be appointed as Personal Representative. Court battles are expensive, emotionally as well as financially. Before you decide to distance yourself from the Probate procedure, consult with an attorney experienced in Probate matters for an opinion about the best way to administer the Estate.

MONIES OWED TO THE DECEDENT

Suppose you owed money to the decedent. Do you need to pay that debt now that he is dead? That depends on whether there is some written document that says the debt is forgiven once the decedent dies. For example, suppose the decedent lent you money to buy your home. If he left a Will saying that once he dies, your debt is forgiven, then you do not need to make any more payments. If you signed a promissory note and mortgage at the time you borrowed the money from the decedent, then the Personal Representative should sign the original promissory note "**PAID IN FULL**" and return the note to you. If the mortgage was recorded, then the Personal Representative should sign and record a satisfaction of mortgage.

If you owed the decedent money and there is no Will, or if there is a Will, no mention of forgiving the debt, then you still owe the money. Monies borrowed from the decedent and his spouse need to be repaid to the spouse. Monies borrowed from the decedent only, become an asset to the Estate of the decedent, meaning that you owe the money to the decedent's Estate. If you are one of the beneficiaries of the Estate, you can deduct the money from your inheritance.

For example, suppose your father left $70,000 in a bank account to be divided equally between you and your two brothers. If you owed your father $20,000, then your father's Estate is really worth $90,000. Instead of paying the $20,000, you can agree to receive $10,000 and have the $20,000 debt forgiven. Each of your brothers will then receive $30,000 in cash.

Who Are The Beneficiaries? 5

A question that comes up early on is who is entitled to the property of the decedent. To answer the question you first need to know how the property was titled (owned) as of the date of death.

There are three ways to own property. The decedent could have owned property jointly with another person; or in trust for another person; or the decedent could have owned property that was titled in his name only.

In general, upon the decedent's death:

> **Joint Property with Rights of Survivorship**
> belongs to the surviving joint owner.
>
> **Trust Property** belongs to the beneficiary
> of the Trust.
>
> Property owned by the **decedent only** is inherited
> by the beneficiaries named in the Will.
> If there is no Will, then the property goes to his heirs
> according to Virginia's Laws of Descent and Distribution.
>
> NOTE ⇨ If the decedent was married, then his
> spouse may have rights in his property.

This chapter describes each type of ownership in detail.

PROPERTY HELD JOINTLY

Bank accounts, securities, motor vehicles, real property can all be owned jointly by two or more people. If one of the joint owners dies, then the survivor(s) continue to own their share of the property. Who owns the share belonging to the decedent depends on how the joint ownership was set up. If the title to the account says that there is a *joint account with survivorship,* then should one of them die, the remaining owner(s) own the property.

If there is no right of survivorship, then the share of the property that belongs to the decedent goes to whomever he named in his Will. If there is no Will, then the decedent's share goes to his next of kin as defined by Virginia's Laws of Intestate Succession (see page 106).

THE JOINT BANK ACCOUNT

Joint accounts opened in Virginia after July 1, 2000 must clearly state JOINT ACCOUNTS WITH SURVIVORSHIP or JOINT ACCOUNT — NO SURVIVORSHIP. Accounts opened prior to that date, or out of state accounts , might not be so specific. The word "Joint" or "Jointly," without any indication of survivorship, does not necessarily mean that the money belongs to the surviving owners. If you have any question about whether there is a right of survivorship, then ask the bank to show you the contract that was signed by the decedent when the account was opened (VA 6.1-125.1, 6.1-125.15).

Each owner of a joint account owns as much of the account as was contributed by that person to the account. It is presumed that a married couple each own half of their joint account, regardless of who deposited the funds. If a survivorship account is held in three names and one owner dies, then the share owned by the decedent is divided equally between the surviving owners. Of course, either owner can go to the bank and withdraw all of the funds in the account. With such an arrangement, the surviving owners need to cooperate with each other to divide the funds in the account equitably. Whoever withdraws the money needs to keep in mind that the Personal Representative can require that the decedent's share of the account be used to pay taxes or monies owed by the decedent (see page 80) (VA 6.1-125.3, 6.1-125.5, 61-125.10).

JOINTLY HELD SECURITIES

You can determine whether the decedent owns a security alone or jointly with another by examining the face of the stock or bond certificate. If two names are printed on the certificate as joint owners with rights of survivorship, or if you see the initials "JTWRS" then the surviving owner can either cash in the security or ask the company to issue a new certificate in the name of the surviving owner, again understanding that the Personal Representative has 6 months to ask that the decedent's share of the securities be used to pay his bills.

Each state has its own securities regulations. If a security held in two or more names, was registered or purchased in another state, then you will need to contact the company to determine how the account was set up; i.e. with or without rights of survivorship.

JOINTLY HELD MOTOR VEHICLE

If a motor vehicle is held jointly, the name of each owner is printed on the title to the motor vehicle. If the names are followed with *or the survivor*, then if one person dies, the survivor owns the car, 100%. If you are such surviving joint owner then you need to go to your local Department of Motor Vehicles to change title and registration. You may wish to call first and determine what documents you will need to take with you.

It is important to change title as soon as you are able. You might be able to get a reduced insurance rate if there is only one person insured under the policy. Also, should the surviving owner be involved in an accident, and title has officially been changed, then there is no question that the estate of the decedent is in no way liable for the accident.

If title to the car was held jointly but there are no rights of survivorship, then the decedent's share of the car goes to his estate in the same manner as a motor vehicle held in the decedent's name only.

MOTOR VEHICLE IN DECEDENT'S NAME ONLY

If the decedent left a Will, then the car goes to the beneficiaries named in the Will. If the decedent died without a Will then the car goes to the next of kin as defined in the Virginia Laws of Descent and Distribution. See page 108 for an explanation of the law.

See Chapter 6 for an explanation of how to transfer title to the proper beneficiary.

VIRGINIA REAL PROPERTY HELD JOINTLY

The name of the owner of real property is printed on the face of the deed. To determine whether the decedent owned the property jointly with another person, you need to look at the last recorded deed. See page 66 if you cannot locate the deed. The first paragraph of the deed should identify the person who transferred the property (the **Grantor**) and the person to whom the property was transferred (the **Grantee**) (VA 55-48).

This deed made the 14th day of August, 2000
between ROBERT TRAYNOR, a single man
hereinafter referred to as the GRANTOR
and
SUSAN CODY, a married woman
and HENRY TRAYNOR, a single man,
as co-owners with right of survivorship
hereinafter referred to as the GRANTEE

Robert Traynor is the Grantor of the deed. That means he transferred the property to Susan Cody and Henry Traynor who are the Grantees and the present owners of the property. Robert transferred the property to Susan and Henry as co-owners *with right of survivorship*. Should one of them die, the other will own the property 100%. The survivor need do nothing to establish the ownership, but both names remain on the deed. In the next chapter we will explain what documents should be recorded to let everyone know that there is just one remaining owner (VA 64.1-104.1).

🖹 DEED WITH A LIFE ESTATE

A *life estate* interest in real property means that the person who owns the life estate has the right to live in that property until he/she dies. You can identify a life estate interest by examining the face of the deed. If somewhere on the face of the deed you see the phrase RESERVING A LIFE ESTATE to the decedent, then the Grantee(s) now own the property. For example, suppose the granting paragraph of the deed reads:

> PETER REILLY, a single man, Grantor
> and ROSE SMITH, a married woman, Grantee
>
> Witnesseth: that . . . the said Grantor,
>   doth grant unto the said Grantee,
>   all the property described as . . .
>
> RESERVING A LIFE ESTATE TO THE GRANTOR

Peter Reilly is the owner of the life estate. While he is alive, the Grantee (Rose Smith) has no right to occupy the property. Once Peter dies, Rose owns the property, and is free to take possession of the property or transfer it, as she sees fit.

As with a survivorship tenancy, nothing need be done to establish Rose's ownership of the property, however documentation should be recorded to shows anyone who is examining title to the property that Rose now owns the property.

▤ DEED HELD AS HUSBAND AND WIFE

If a married couple hold property as follows:
TODD AMES AND SUSAN AMES, TENANTS BY THE ENTIRETIES
or
TODD AMES AND SUSAN AMES, TENANTS BY THE ENTIRETY
then when one spouse dies, and providing they are married at the time of death, the surviving spouse owns the property 100%. As with joint tenancy with right of survivor, documents will need to be recorded so that anyone who is examining title to the property will know that the surviving spouse is now the sole owner of the property. The next Chapter explains what documents need to be recorded (VA 55-20, 55-20.1).

 **LAWYER**   DIVORCED PRIOR TO DEATH

Once a couple divorce all property (both real property and personal property) held by the couple as a Tenancy by the Entirety becomes a Tenancy In Common (VA 20-111).

If the decedent was divorced before he died, and he still holds property together former spouse, then unless the Final Judgment states otherwise, the former spouse has no right of survivorship in that property. The decedent's half of the property descends to his heirs or beneficiaries and not to his former spouse.

▤ DEED HELD AS TENANTS IN COMMON

If the Grantee of a deed identifies the decedent and another as **TENANTS IN COMMON** then the decedent's share belongs to whomever the decedent named as his beneficiary in his Will. If the decedent died without a Will, then the Virginia Laws of Descent and Distribution determine who inherits the property.

If the deed names two or more people as joint owners but does not specify Right of Survivorship, then according to Virginia law, they hold title as Tenants in Common. Similarly if property is deeded to a husband and wife and does not say "with Right of Survivorship" or does not indicate that they hold the property as Tenants by the Entirety, then they hold title as Tenants In Common (VA 55-20).

 **LAWYER**   THE AMBIGUOUS DEED

Most deeds clearly state whether the joint owners of the property intend a surviving owner to inherit the decedent's share. But some deeds are not all that descriptive. For example, a deed granted to
   "Harry Simms and Audra Simms, his wife, jointly"
is confusing. If the Grantor intended the Simms to have rights of survivorship, then the wording of the deed does not live up to the letter of the law. Depending on the facts of the case, it may be that the surviving spouse does not inherit the decedent's share. Best to consult with an attorney if you have any question about how to interpret the deed.

 **LAWYER** | OUT OF STATE PROPERTY

This chapter relates only to property owned by the decedent in the state of Virginia. If the decedent owned property in another state or country, then the laws of that state or country determine who inherits that property. The laws of each state are similar, but not the same. For example, in many states a Tenancy by the Entirety is created merely by having the Grantee identified as "Husband and Wife." Other states such as Wisconsin, do not recognize a Tenancy by the Entirety. In such states, a married couple holds property as Tenants In Common, unless the deed specifically states that there are rights of survivorship.

If the decedent owned real property in another state, then it is important to consult with an attorney in that state to determine who owns the property now that the Grantee is dead.

 This discussion on the different types of ownership of real property presumes that you are in possession of the most recent, valid deed. The decedent could have signed another, later, deed. Before you come to a conclusion about who inherits the property it is advisable to have an attorney or a title company do a title search to determine the owner of the property as of the decedent's date of death.

PROPERTY HELD IN TRUST

BANK/ SECURITY ACCOUNTS

If a bank account or security account is registered in the name of the decedent held "in trust for" or "for the benefit of" someone. Once the bank has a certified copy of the death certificate, the bank will turn over the account to the beneficiary.

If the bank or security account is registered in the name of the decedent "as Trustee under a Trust agreement," that means the decedent was the Trustee of a Trust and the bank will turn over that account to the Successor Trustee of the Trust. Banks usually require a copy of the Trust agreement when the account was opened, so the bank probably knows the identity of the Successor Trustee. If the Trust was amended to name a different Successor Trustee, you need to present the bank with a copy of that amendment together with a certified copy of the death certificate.

If there is no Successor Trustee, then the bank will give the property to the beneficiaries identified in the Trust. If no beneficiary survives the Trustee, then the property will be given to the decedent's Personal Representative, to be included in the decedent's Probate Estate (VA 6.1-125.12)

MOTOR VEHICLE

If the motor vehicle is held in the name of the decedent "as Trustee," then the motor vehicle continues to be Trust property. The Successor Trustee will need to contact the motor vehicle bureau to have title changed to that of the Successor Trustee. If the Trust agreement directs the Successor Trustee to sell the car or to distribute that car to a beneficiary, then the Successor Trustee will need to arrange to have this done. See Chapter 6 for directions about how to transfer the car to a new owner.

REAL PROPERTY

If the decedent had a Trust and put property that he owned into the Trust, then the deed may read something like this:

This deed made the 14th day of August, 2000
between JOHN ZAMORA
and MARIA ZAMORA, GRANTOR
and
JOHN ZAMORA, **Trustee of the**
JOHN ZAMORA TRUST AGREEMENT
DATED FEBRUARY 26, 2000, GRANTEE
. . .

The death of the Trustee of a Trust does not change the ownership of the property. It remains in the Trust. The Trust document might say whether the person who takes John's place as Trustee (the Successor Trustee) should sell or keep the property or perhaps give it to a beneficiary. If no instruction is given, the Successor Trustee can use his discretion as to what to do with the property. If you are a beneficiary of the Trust and you are concerned about what the Successor Trustee will do with the property, then it is best to consult with your attorney to learn about your rights under that Trust.

THE DEED OF TRUST

A Deed of Trust is very different from the above described deed. The Deed of Trust is essentially a mortgage. The owner of the property places title to the property with a Trustee as security for payment of monies owed to the lender. If the debt is not paid, then the Trustee (after proper foreclosure on the property) will deliver title to the property to the Beneficiary of the Deed of Trust, namely the lender (VA 55-59).

PROPERTY IN DECEDENT'S NAME ONLY

If the decedent owned property that was in his name only (not jointly with rights of survivorship, or in trust for someone), then some sort of Probate procedure will be necessary before the heirs can get possession of that property. Who is entitled to the decedent's Probate Estate depends on whether the decedent died with or without a Will. If the decedent died *testate* (with a Will) then the beneficiaries of the decedent's property are identified in the Will.

If the decedent died *intestate* (without a Will) his Probate Estate is distributed according to the Laws of Intestate Succession. These laws determine who inherits the decedent's intestate Probate Estate and what percentage of the Estate each heir is to receive once all the bills and costs of administering the Estate are paid.

The law recognizes the right of the family to inherit the decedent's property. The law covers all possible relationships beginning with the decedent's spouse.

Who's The Spouse?

In this era of people challenging the concept of the family unit, those of a philosophical bent may ponder the meaning of marriage. Is it a union of two people in the eyes of God? Is it even a union? Maybe it is just a contract between two people. The Commonwealth of Virginia does not concern itself with such things. If a person dies intestate, then the state will distribute the property according to the laws of the Virginia; and the laws of Virginia determine whether two people are married.

MARRIED IN VIRGINIA

To be married in Virginia means that a man and a woman have obtained a license to marry from the state, solemnized the marriage by a state or religious ceremony, and then lived together as man and wife. Virginia law specifically prohibits the marriage of people:

- ☒ who are currently married to another person;
- ☒ who are ancestors or descendants of each other ; i.e., parent-child, grandparent-child, etc.
- ☒ who are aunt and nephew or uncle and niece regardless of whether related through half or whole blood;
- ☒ who are brother and sister. This includes adopted siblings, regardless of fact that they are not blood relatives (VA 20-38.1).

The law does not bar marriages between cousins.

THE COMMON LAW MARRIAGE

A common law marriage is one that has not been solemnized by ceremony. The couple agree to live together as man and wife, and then publicly hold themselves out as being married. Many states, including Virginia, do not recognize a common law marriage as being valid, and have passed laws to that effect (VA 20-13).

SAME SEX MARRIAGES

Vermont is the first state to recognize same sex marriages, which they refer to as a "civil union." Several other states (including Virginia) have passed statutes, specifically denying marital status to couples of the same gender regardless of whether that marriage is valid in any other state or country (VA 20-45.2).

If you have any question about the validity of the decedent's marriage, then it is important to consult with an attorney.

VIRGINIA'S LAWS OF DESCENT

If the decedent neglected to make a Will, then the state of Virginia provides one for him in the Virginia *Laws of Descent and Distribution*. These laws are also referred to as the *Laws of Intestate Succession*. The statute makes a distinction between real and personal property. *Real property* is land and whatever is growing on or permanently attached to the land, such as a house. *Personal property* is everything else (money, securities cars, paintings, etc.). If the decedent died without a Will, then his Probate Estate is distributed as follows:

✧ MARRIED, NO CHILD OR ALL CHILDREN OF DECEDENT

If at the time of death the decedent was married and had no surviving *lineal descendants* (child, grandchild, great-grandchild, etc.) — or — if all of the decedent's descendents are those of his spouse, then all of his Probate Estate (real or personal) goes to the surviving spouse.

✧ CHILD, NO SPOUSE

If the decedent was single, then his children inherit the Probate Estate, in equal shares, *per stirpes*, meaning that if all of the decedent's children are alive, they each take an equal share of the probate estate; but if one child dies before the decedent, then the share intended for the deceased child is given to the his/her children, in equal shares. If the deceased child died without lineal descendants, then the surviving children divide the Probate Estate equally between them (VA 64.1-1, 64.1-3, 64.1-11).

✧ MARRIED, CHILD NOT OF SURVIVING SPOUSE

If decedent was survived a descendant who is not a descendant of his surviving spouse, then the spouse gets 1/3rd of his real property. His children share equally in the remaining 2/3rds, in equal shares, per stirpes. As for the decedent's personal property, the spouse is entitled to keep up to $10,000 as Exempt Property. The remaining personal property is divided with 1/3rd going to the spouse and the remaining 2/3rds to the decedent's children, in equal shares, per stirpes.

✧ NO CHILD, NO SPOUSE

If the decedent had no spouse or lineal descendant, then his property is divided equally between his parents. If only one of his parents is alive, then all of the property goes to that parent. If neither parent is alive, then the estate goes to the decedent's brothers and sisters in equal shares, per stirpes.

If the decedent had no brothers, sisters, nephews or nieces, then the Probate Estate is divided with half going to the decedent's grandparents (or to the survivor) on his mother's side. If neither maternal grandparent is alive, the property goes to their lineal descendants in equal shares, per stirpes. If there are no lineal descendants, then the entire Probate Estate goes to the paternal grandparents (or their next of kin).

The other half is distributed in the same manner; i.e., half goes to the decedent's grandparents (or to the survivor) father's side. Again, if neither paternal grandparent is alive, then to their lineal descendants in equal shares, per stirpes. If there are no surviving lineal descendants, then the entire Probate estate goes to the maternal grandparents (or their next of kin) (VA 64.1-1).

NO NEXT OF KIN, BUT RELATIVES OF A DECEASED SPOUSE

If a person dies without a Will and he has absolutely no surviving kinfolk, but his deceased spouse has surviving kinfolk, the Probate Estate is distributed as if the spouse was entitled to the entire Probate Estate, and died without a Will.

THE STATE: HEIR OF LAST RESORT

As discussed previously, all unclaimed property goes to the Virginia Department of Treasury, so if a person dies without a Will and he has absolutely no next of kin, or he had a Will and no beneficiary can be found, then the Commonwealth of Virginia "inherits" the decedent's Probate Estate (VA 64.1-12).

RELATIVES OF HALF-BLOOD INHERIT HALF

Relatives of half-blood inherit half as much as a relative of whole blood. For example, if the decedent was survived by a brothers from the same set of parents and a sister with the same father but a different mother, then if the decedent died without a Will, his sister would get half as much as his brother. Specifically, the Probate Estate would be divided into three equal shares. His brother would inherit 2 shares (or 2/3rds of the estate) and his sister would get one share (1/3rd of the estate) (VA 64.1-2).

NEGLECTFUL SPOUSE OR PARENT INHERIT NONE

If the decedent was wilfully deserted or abandoned by his spouse, and the separation continued until the date of death, then the surviving spouse is barred from claiming any statutory right to inherit the decedent's property. This includes exempt property, family and/or homestead allowance, etc. Similarly, if a parent wilfully deserts or abandons a minor or incapacitated child and this continues until the child dies, then the parent is barred from inheriting anything under Virginia's Laws of Descent and Distribution (VA 64.1-16.3)

CAUTION   IT ISN'T ALL THAT SIMPLE

The explanation in this book of the laws of intestate succession is abridged. Even though you may now know more about the Virginia Laws of Descent and Distribution than you ever wanted to know, there is much more to the law. For example, we did not explain in detail exactly how the estate is distributed if the decedent is survived only by descendants of his maternal or paternal grandparents. We could give an example explaining the law, but we thought you might enjoy a puzzle instead:

Winston died intestate leaving $100,000. His only relatives were his Aunt Susie (on his mother's side) and her two children Ramona and Abigail; and on his father's side, a second cousin, Elvis, (the child of a deceased cousin). How much does each relative receive?

You can check your answer by visiting the Virginia section of the Eagle Publishing Company Web site:
            http://www.eaglepublishing.com

Those who tried the above puzzle can appreciate how complex the Laws of Descent and Distribution can be. Unless the descent is straight forward, with the decedent leaving a surviving spouse and/or children (all of whom survive him), it is best to consult with an attorney before you decide who is entitled to inherit the decedent's intestate property.

THE RIGHTS OF A CHILD

ADOPTED CHILD

An adopted child has the same rights to inherit property from his adoptive parents as does a natural child. The adopted child has no right to inherit property from his natural parents unless the adoptive parent is the spouse of the child's natural parent, for example, should the child's mother marry and the stepfather adopt the child, then the child still has the right to inherit from his mother (VA 64.1-5.1).

AFTERBORN CHILD

If a child was conceived prior to the decedent's death, and born after the death, then the child inherits the same as any other natural child of the decedent (VA 64.1-8.1).

NON-MARITAL CHILD

A child born out of wedlock has the same rights to inherit from his/her natural father as does one born in wedlock, provided:

☑ the decedent participated in a marriage ceremony with the child's mother, before or after the birth and regardless of whether the attempted marriage was valid in Virginia - or -

☑ paternity was established by clear and convincing evidence.

If the decedent denied his paternity, then it will take a court procedure to establish (or disprove) paternity. To inherit property from the decedent, the child, or someone acting on behalf of the child, will need to file an *affidavit* (a sworn, written statement) with the Clerk stating that the decedent is the child's parent; and at the same time file a petition in an appropriate Court asking to have the Court determine whether the decedent was the child's father (VA 64.1-5.1).

THE CHILD OF AN ASSISTED CONCEPTION

Medical technology has made important contributions to solving the problem of infertility. There are all sorts of solutions, from hormone replacement therapy, to sperm banks that provide donations anonymously, to frozen sperm and/or ova to be thawed and used at a later date, to women who become a surrogate or gestational mother.

Solving a set of medical problems has opened the door to a new set of legal problems. Used to be, the only question was "Who's the father?"

Now it could well be "Who's the mother?

To answer these questions, the Commonwealth of Virginia has passed laws (VA 20-156 to 20-165) to legally establish the parentage of children whose conception was assisted by medical technology. Two major problems are the case of a woman who has an assisted conception without the knowledge and/or consent of her spouse; and the case of a child that was born from a surrogate mother.

We will examine the law as it relates to the right of the child to inherit property.

Under Virginia law, if a child is born to parents using any form of assisted conception, then that child has the same rights as a child born the old fashioned way, with the following exceptions:

FERTILIZATION AFTER DEATH

Increasingly people are having their sperm or ovum preserved in a frozen state until such time as they wish to become a parent. For example, suppose a man has been diagnosed with cancer and he fears that the cancer treatment may cause genetic damage. He may decide to have his sperm frozen until he is well and decides to have children. Should he decide to use the sperm at a later date, then that child is his, just as any other child he may have. A problem can arise, if he dies and his surviving spouse decides to use that sperm, and his family objects to the procedure.

Virginia legislature recognizes that they cannot stop a pregnancy once fertilization takes place, but they can determine the rights and responsibilities of the parties. Under Virginia law, if a sperm or ovum is preserved, and the donor dies before fertilization takes place, then the deceased donor is not the parent of the child unless:

(a) the procedure took place before there was reasonable notice of the death - or -

(b) the donor agreed, in writing, to be the parent before the implantation (VA 20-158, 64.1-8.1).

If, under Virginia law, the deceased donor is not the parent, the child cannot inherit anything from the donor or his family.

FATHER DID NOT CONSENT TO PROCEDURE

If a wife uses any form of assisted conception without the knowledge or consent of her spouse, then the husband has the right to ask a court to terminate all of his parental rights and responsibilities. He must do this within two years after he discovered (or reasonably should have discovered) that she used assisted conception. If the husband is successful, then the child cannot inherit from his father, and vis-versa, the father and his family cannot inherit from the child (VA 20-158).

BIRTH AS A RESULT OF A SURROGACY CONTRACT

Virginia statute 20-160 gives the intended parents and the gestational parents, the opportunity to have a Court approve their surrogacy contract. If the parties get Court approval, then within 60 days of the child's birth, a new birth certificate is issued by the State Registrar, naming the intended parents as the child's parents.

If the parties do not obtain Court approval of the surrogacy contract, then things get complex, especially if the surrogate has a change of heart. It is beyond the scope of this book to go into all of the "what ifs." (The statute is fairly simple to read if you are interested.) We'll just take the best case scenario where all of the parties live up to the surrogate agreement. In that case, if one of the intended parents is also a genetic parent, i.e., one of them contributed a sperm or ovum, then they can ask the Court to have a new birth certificate issued naming the intended parents as the child's parents.

If neither of the intended parents is a genetic parent, then the parties need to go through an adoption procedure. Once the procedure is complete, the child has the same right to inherit as does any adopted child (VA 20-159, 20-160, 20-162).

WHO DIED FIRST?

Virginia statute requires that a heir survive the decedent by at least 120 hours (5 days) in order to inherit property according to the Virginia's Laws of Descent and Distribution. If an heir does not live for at least 5 days after the decedent's death, then the decedent's property is distributed as if the heir died first. This rule also applies to property inherited by Will, unless the Will makes some different provision. The rule does not apply if it would result in the Commonwealth taking the property.

Sometimes it happens that two family members die simultaneously, and no one knows who died first. For example, suppose a husband and wife die together in an car crash, how is their property distributed? Virginia's Uniform Simultaneous Death Act solves the problem. The law provides that each person is assumed to have survived the other and the property of each is distributed on that basis. For example, suppose the husband is insured, with his wife as beneficiary. The proceeds of the policy are distributed as if the wife died before her husband. The proceeds will be given to the alternate beneficiary named in the policy. If no alternate beneficiary was named, the proceeds of the policy will go to the insured party (in this case, the husband).

Property owned jointly by the couple, with no provision for who is to inherit the property should they both die, is divided with half going to the Estate of the husband and the other half to the Estate of the wife. If they each have a Will, the husband's half is distributed according to his Will and the wife's half according to her Will. If they die without a Will, then the husband's half is distributed according to Virginia's Descent and Distribution as if he were single; and vis-versa (VA 64.1-104.2, 64.1-104.3, 64.1-104.4 64.1-104.6).

WHEN TO CHALLENGE THE WILL

It is not uncommon for a family member to be unhappy with the way the decedent willed his property. If you are tempted to challenge a Will, first consider whether the Will is valid under Virginia law.

In Virginia, a Will is presumed to be valid if at the time the decedent made the Will:

➢ he was at least 18 years of age

➢ he was of sound mind

Virginia courts have ruled that a person making a Will is acting with sound mind if at the time he made the Will:

☑ he knew what he was doing (namely making a Will)

- and -

☑ he knew what property he had

- and -

☑ he knew how he wanted to dispose of his property

- and -

☑ he remembered and understood his relationship to his family members and what claims they might have upon him.

(*Fields v. Fields*, 255 Va. 546 (1998), 499 S.E.2D 826).

Virginia statute requires that the Will be in writing and signed by the person who is making the Will in the presence of two people who sign the Will as witness.

No witness is necessary if the decedent wrote the Will in his own hand and then signed it, providing that two people who have no interest in the Will can prove to the Court that the decedent did, in fact, write the Will (VA 64.1-49).

THE UNWITNESSED WILL

The first step in the probate procedure is to have the Probate court determine whether the Will presented is valid. If the Will is in writing and signed by the Will maker in the presence of at least two credible witnesses, then there should be no problem in having the Will accepted into Probate. If the Will is notarized, then the Court will probably not require further proof. If the Will is witnessed but not notarized, then the court will ask the witnesses to testify that they saw the Will maker sign the Will.

But suppose the decedent wrote out a Will in his own hand and signed it with no one present? Such a Will is called a *holographic Will.* Many states refuse to accept a holographic Will into probate. But in Virginia, the Probate Court will accept a holographic Will, provided two independent witnesses (i.e., who have no interest in the Will) testify that the handwriting was that of the decedent (VA 64.1-49).

The problem with a holographic Will, in this or any other state, is its authenticity. Because no one saw the decedent sign the Will, it is hard to determine whether the Will was written by the decedent or is a forgery.

If all the decedent left was a holographic Will, then you need to consult with an attorney experienced in Probate matters, to present evidence to the court that the Will does (or does not) qualify as a holographic Will in the state of Virginia.

THE VERBAL WILL

Picture a death bed scene. The elderly gentleman is surrounded by several family members. In a whisper, just audible enough to be heard, he says:

"Even though I am a wealthy man, I never got around to making a Will. You all have been good to me, but I did want my entire fortune to go to my nephew, Robert. He has been like a son to me. "

Do you think Robert can inherit his Uncle's estate?

Not in Virginia unless:
⇨ Someone writes down his uncle's wishes, and
⇨ The uncle acknowledges that this is his Will, and
⇨ The uncle tells someone to sign the Will for him, and
⇨ The person does so, and two people sign the Will as witnesses (VA 64.1-49).

Considering that the uncle's relatives will probably inherit the fortune under the Virginia Laws of Descent and Distribution, it is doubtful that Robert is in danger of becoming wealthy at any time in the near future.

THE WILL THAT IS CONTRARY TO LAW

Sometimes a person who is of sound mind, makes a Will, but that Will has the effect of giving a spouse less than the spouse is entitled to receive under Virginia law. One such example is that of Nancy. Hers was not an easy life. She divorced her hard drinking first husband. The final judgment gave her their homestead, some securities and sole custody of their daughter. After the divorce, Nancy had her attorney prepare a Will leaving all she owned to her daughter. She had the attorney change the deed to her name and her daughter as joint tenants with rights of survivorship.

Some years later Nancy met and married Harry. The moved into Nancy's house and two years later had a son.

Nancy's son was 5 and her daughter 18, when Nancy died after a lengthy battle with cancer. Just before she died, Nancy gave $20,000 to her daughter to see her through the first year of college. She also spoke about her Will "My Will leaves everything to you. I didn't bother to change it because your stepfather has a good job, and he is a good father, so I know he and your brother will do just fine."

Nancy did not have much when she died — the house, her household furnishings and some personal items. Her securities and bank accounts were worth about $50,000.

When the funeral was over, Harry discovered the Will (leaving all to his stepdaughter). He also found the cancelled $20,000 check, but the thing that made him ballistic, was having his stepdaughter tell him that she was putting the house up for sale, and he would have to move out.

Harry went to his attorney.

"I was a good husband to Nancy, supporting and taking care of her all during her illness. It was me, and not her daughter, who was at her side when she died. Don't I have any rights? And what about my son? Doesn't he have any rights?"

"Your son was born after Nancy made her Will. Under Virginia statute 64.1-71, he is entitled to as much as his sister receives or as much as he would have received if your wife died without a Will — which ever is the lesser value. You also have many rights provided you did not give up those rights. Virginia statute 64.1-151.6 allows you to waive their rights by signing a pre-nuptial or post-nuptial agreement. Did you sign any such document?"

"Absolutely not!"

"In that case, under Virginia statute 64.1-13, 64.1-16, you are entitled to an *elective share* of her estate, which is essentially one-third of her estate, plus you and your son are also entitled to Exempt property, a Family Allowance and a Homestead Allowance."

Harry was still upset "But her house is worth the most amount of money. She made her daughter joint owner with rights of survivorship. Don't I have Dower rights or something?"

"Dower rights are for widows. Curtesy rights are for widowers. But in Virginia those rights were abolished in 1991, long before you were married. Virginia statute does give you the right to continue to live in the homestead until the Court determines your rights in the family residence. And you can stay there until the Court ruling without paying anything for rent, taxes, repairs or insurance" (VA 64.1-19.2, 64.1-16.4).

Harry said "And what about the $20,000 she gave to her daughter just before she died?"

"If within the five years preceding her death, your wife made a gift of more than $10,000 to anyone without your consent, then you are to receive one-third of any amount that exceeded $10,000. In this case, your stepdaughter needs to give you $3,333.33."

Harry doubted that his stepdaughter would surrender the money willingly "How can we convince my stepdaughter to return the money to me?"

The attorney said "The Court will decide who is entitled to what. The elective share is not automatic. The Court will hold a hearing and determine whether you have a right to that money. Your stepdaughter will have an opportunity to voice any objection she may have. If the Court determines that you are entitled to the money, then the court will decide how it is to be paid. You will need to sign a petition (request) which I will prepare that requests your elective share. I will file it with the Clerk of the Circuit Court. We need to do this within 6 months of the filing of the Will or the appointment of a Personal Representative, whichever date is later." (VA 64.1-13. 64.1-16.2).

Nancy's daughter did not fare as well as her mother intended. There was no cash left in the estate after the funeral expenses, medical bills, the family allowance and homestead allowance were paid. All she inherited was the house, and she had to pay her stepfather part of the proceeds of the sale to make up for his share of the $20,000 given to her before her mother died.

No doubt Nancy did not understand what would happen to her estate once she passed on. The Will she left did not accomplish her goal of providing for her son. All it did was cause turmoil and an irreparable rift between Harry and Richard. It didn't need to be that way. Had Nancy known about Virginia law, she could have consulted with an attorney and set up an estate plan that could have provided for her daughter, without alienating her husband.

But, the moral of the story, for the purpose of this discussion, is that if you believe that the decedent's Will is not valid or is not drafted according to Virginia law, then you need to consult with an attorney experienced in probate matters to determine your legal rights under that Will.

Getting Possession Of The Property 6

Knowing who is entitled to receive the decedent's property is one thing. Getting that property is another. As explained in the previous chapter if the decedent held property jointly with someone, or in a Trust for someone, the property now belongs to the joint owner or beneficiary. If it is personal property such as a bank account or a security, the beneficiary can usually get possession of the property by giving a certified copy of the death certificate to the financial institution.

If the decedent held real or personal property in his name only, or as a Tenant In Common, then some sort of Probate procedure may be required in order to transfer ownership to the proper beneficiary. If a full Probate procedure is necessary, then you will need the assistance of an attorney. But there are many items that can be transferred without legal assistance. This chapter explains how to get possession of such items.

This chapter also contains an explanation of the different kinds of Probate procedure and when it is appropriate to use that procedure.

DISTRIBUTING PERSONAL PROPERTY

Too often, the first person to discover the body will help himself to the decedent's *personal effects* (clothing, jewelry, appliances, electrical equipment, cameras, books, household items and furnishing, etc.). Unless that person is the decedent's sole beneficiary, such action is unconscionable, if not illegal.

If the decedent was married and did not have children, then all of the decedent's personal effects belong to his spouse unless he left a Will giving a particular item of personal property to someone else. The decedent may have left a separate writing giving some personal item to someone. Under Virginia law, a person can leave any of his personal effects (not money) by means of a separate writing, providing the writing was signed by him (VA 64.1-45.1).

If the decedent was not married, then all of his personal effects should be given to the person appointed as the Personal Representative. The Representative then has the duty to distribute the property according to the decedent's Will, or if the decedent died intestate, according to the Virginia Rules of Descent and Distribution.

If you determine that there is no need for a Probate procedure and the decedent did not have a Will then his next of kin need to divide all of the personal effects among themselves in approximately equal proportions. Most personal effects have little, if any, monetary value. Furniture may be worth less than it costs to ship. In such case, the beneficiaries may decide to donate the personal property to the decedent's favorite charity.

What's Equal?

The decedent's Will or if no Will, then the Virginia Laws of Descent and Distribution may direct that the decedent's personal property be divided equally between two or more beneficiaries. The problem with the term "equal" is that people have different ideas of what "equal" means. Unless there is clear evidence that the decedent's Will meant something else, "equal" refers to the monetary value of the item and not to the number of items received. For example, to divide the decedent's personal effects equally, one beneficiary may receive an expensive item of jewelry and another beneficiary may receive several items whose overall value is approximately equal to that single piece of jewelry.

When distributing personal effects there needs to be cooperation and perhaps compromise, or else bitter arguments might arise over items of little monetary value.

One such argument occurred when an elderly woman died who was rich only in her love for her five children and 12 grandchildren. After the funeral, the children gathered in their mother's apartment. Each child had his/her own furnishings and no need for anything in the apartment. They agreed to donate all of their mother's personal effects to a local charity with the exception of a few items of sentimental value.

Each child took some small item as a remembrance —
a handkerchief, a large platter that their mother used to
serve family dinners, a doily their mother crocheted.
Things went smoothly until it came to her photograph
album. Frank, the youngest sibling, said, "I'll take this."
Marie objected saying, "But there are pictures in that
album that I want."

Frank retorted, "You already took all the pictures Mom
had on her dresser."

The argument went downhill from there. Unsettled
sibling rivalries boiled over, fueled by the hurt of the loss
that they were all experiencing.

It almost came to blows when the eldest settled the
argument: "Frank you make copies of all of the photos in
the album for Marie. Marie, you make copies of all of the
pictures that you took and give them to Frank. This way
you both will have a complete set of Mom's pictures.

And while you're at it, make copies for the rest of us."

THE SMALL ESTATE AFFIDAVIT

Virginia law allows people who have possession of the decedent's personal property to turn the property over to the decedent's spouse, or if no spouse, then to whoever is entitled to the property under Virginia law, provided the total value of the property transferred in not greater than $15,000. The beneficiary can get possession of the item by giving the person who holds the property a **SMALL ESTATE AFFIDAVIT.** To use the Small Estate Affidavit, the following facts must be true:

☑ The net value of the decedent's personal property is not greater than $15,000.

☑ No Probate procedure is pending.

☑ Sixty days have passed since the death.

It is appropriate to use the Affidavit to get possession of property such as:

⇨ bank accounts and certificates of deposit;

⇨ state income tax refund;

⇨ securities (stocks, bonds, mutual funds, etc.)

⇨ final wages due to the decedent;

⇨ money or property held by a municipally operated health care facility;

⇨ tangible personal property (clothing, jewelry, etc.)

If the sum of the items to be transferred is greater than $10,000, then you cannot use the Small Estate Affidavit and will need to go through a full Probate procedure (VA 6.1-71, 64.1-123, 64.1-123.1, 64.1-124.1).

There is an example of the Small Estate Affidavit on the next page. You can pick up a copy of the Affidavit from the Clerk of the Probate Court.

AFFIDAVIT UNDER VIRGINIA SMALL ESTATES ACT 64.1-132.2

_____

COMMONWEALTH OF VIRGINIA

The Affiant _____, first being duly sworn deposes and says that:

1. The decedent_____ died on _____, a resident of _____ county, Virginia.

2. The value of the entire personal Probate estate, wherever located, does not exceed $15,000.

3. At least 60 days has elapsed since the death of the decedent.

4. No application for the appointment of a personal representative is pending or has been granted in any jurisdiction.

5. The Will (if testate) was Probated and a list of heirs required by section 64.1-134 has been duly filed as of _____ in the Clerk's Office of _____ County, Virginia.

6. The following person(s) are the heirs under law or if testate, the beneficiary under the terms of the Last Will and Testament, and are entitled to delivery of the property:

_____

_____

_____

I, _____, state to the best of my knowledge and belief the above figures reflect the estimated value of the decedent's estate as of the date of his/her death.

_____

AFFIANT

Subscribed and sworn to before me by _____ this day _____.

_____

Deputy Clerk/Notary Public

My commission expires _____

COMPLETING THE AFFIDAVIT

Notice that if the decedent had a Will, then before trying to get possession of the property, you need to file the Will with the Clerk of the Probate Court, and fill out a form that identifies all of the beneficiaries. If more than one person is entitled to get possession of the personal property, then all should sign the Affidavit in the presence of a Notary Public, or in the presence of the Clerk.

The Affidavit also states that no Personal Representative has been appointed. If it later happens that a full Probate procedure is necessary, and a Personal Representative is appointed, then you may need to turn over the property to the person who is appointed as Personal Representative (VA 64.1-132.3).

MAKING THE TRANSFER

You may save yourself time by first calling the person in possession of the property and finding out what they will require in order to turn over the property to you. For example, if you are trying to close out a bank account, then make an appointment to meet someone who has authority to make the transfer. Ask whether they will require a certified copy of the death certificate, or proof of your identity. If there is a Will, ask whether they may want to see a certified copy of the Will.

It could happen that the person who has possession of the property refuses to turn it over to you regardless of what document you offer. If that happens, you need to go to the Probate Court and get a Personal Representative appointed who will have authority, under order of the Court, to take possession of all of the decedent's property.

As discussed in Chapter 3, if the decedent had his primary residence in another state, but had property in this state then the initial Probate procedure may be conducted in the state of his residence or here in Virginia. If the initial Probate procedure is conducted in Virginia, then the Personal Representative will handle the transfer of the property. If the initial Probate procedure is conducted in another state, the person appointed as Personal Representative in that state may be able to transfer the decedent's personal property without going through another Probate procedure here. If the Virginia property is less than $10,000, then whoever is holding the property can turn it over to the Personal Representative after 90 days — provided no one else claims it.

If the decedent's personal property is $10,000 or more, then the Personal Representative must publish notice once a week for 4 successive weeks in a paper of general circulation in the city or county where the property is located. The notice must state that the Personal Representative intends to take possession of the property. If no one comes forward to make claim to the property, then after 90 days the property can be transferred to the out of state Personal Representative (VA 64.1-130).

Regardless of the value of the Virginia property, if the person holding the property refuses to give it up, or if someone makes claim to the property and the matter cannot be resolved, it may be necessary to conduct an ancillary Probate procedure, and let the Virginia Court decide the matter.

INCOME TAX REFUNDS

Any refund due to the decedent under a joint federal income tax return filed by his surviving spouse will be sent to the surviving spouse. If the decedent's Personal Representative filed the final return, then the refund check will be sent to him to be deposited to the estate account.

If the decedent was single and no Probate procedure is necessary, then whoever is entitled to the decedent's estate is entitled to the refund check. If you are the beneficiary of the decedent's estate, you can obtain the refund by filing IRS form 1310 along with the decedent's final income tax return (the 1040). You can obtain form 1310 from the decedent's accountant, or if he did not have an accountant and you wish to file yourself, you can call the IRS at (800) 829-3676 to obtain the form.

You can get instructions, publications and forms from the Internal Revenue Service Web site:

 IRS WEB SITE
IRS FORMS AND INSTRUCTIONS
http://www.irs.ustreas.gov/prod/forms_pubs/forms.html
IRS PUBLICATIONS
http://www.irs.ustreas.gov/prod/forms_pubs/pubs.html

The Personal Representative does not need to file form 1310 because once he files the decedent's final income tax return, any refund will be forwarded to him. Similarly, it is not necessary for the surviving spouse who filed a joint return to file form 1310.

THE STATE INCOME TAX REFUND

The decedent's final Virginia State income tax return needs to be filed by May 1st in the year following the date of his death. Virginia follows much the same policy as that of the federal government, so whoever files the decedent's federal income tax return needs to file the state income tax return as well. You can get information about filing the final return, by calling (804) 367-8031. You can download forms from the Virginia Department of Taxation Web site:

 VIRGINIA DEPARTMENT OF TAXATION
http://www.tax.state.va.us

If there is a refund due, and that sum does not exceed $10,000, the Small Estate Affidavit can be used to make the transfer to the proper beneficiary.

DEPOSITING THE TAX REFUND
If the refund check is sent to the Personal Representative, then he will deposit it into the estate account. If there is no Probate procedure and the refund check is in the name of the decedent, you can deposit the check into the decedent's bank account. You can obtain all of the money in that account by using whatever Probate procedure is appropriate depending on the value of the estate. If the You can use the Small Estate Affidavit (on page 129) if the value of the decedent's personal property does not exceed $10,000. For values over $10,000 you will need to have a full Probate procedure (see page 143).

TRANSFERRING THE CAR

If the decedent owned a motor vehicle, then title to the car needs to be transferred to the proper beneficiary. The new owner needs to register the car in the state where it will be driven. You may want to limit the use of the car until the transfer is complete. If the decedent's car is involved in an accident before the car is transferred to the new owner, then the decedent's estate may be liable for the damage. Having adequate insurance on the car may save the estate from monetary loss, but a pending lawsuit could delay the Probate procedure and prevent any money from being distributed to the beneficiaries until the lawsuit is settled.

If the car was in the decedent's name only, and there is a Probate procedure then it is the Personal Representative's job to transfer the motor vehicle to the proper beneficiary. If the decedent had a Will and he made a specific gift of the car to someone, then the Personal Representative will transfer the car to that person.

If there was no mention of the car in his Will, and the spouse does not want to take it Exempt Property, then the car goes to the *residuary beneficiaries* under the Will, i.e., those who inherit whatever is left once all the bills have been paid and all the special gifts made in the Will are distributed.

If the decedent did not have a Will, then the car goes to the decedent's heirs as determined by the Virginia Laws of Descent and Distribution, again subject to the right of a surviving spouse to take the car as Exempt Property.

TRANSFER WHEN MORE THAN ONE BENEFICIARY

If there is more than one person who has the right to inherit the car, then they all can take title to the car. That may not be a practical thing to do since only one person can drive the car at any given time and if one gets into an accident, then they all can be held liable. The better route is for the beneficiaries to agree to have one person take title to the car. The person taking title will need to compensate the others for their share of the car. In such case the beneficiaries need to come to an agreement as to the value of the car.

DETERMINING THE VALUE OF THE CAR

Cars are valued in different ways. The **collateral** value of the car is the value that banks use to evaluate the car for purposes of making a loan to the owner of the car. Because banks print these values in book form, the collateral value is also referred to as the **book value** of the car. If you were to trade in a car for the purpose of purchasing a new car, the car dealer would offer you the **wholesale** value of the car. Were you to purchase that same car from a car dealer, he would price it at its **retail** or **fair market value**. Usually the retail price is highest, wholesale is lowest and the book value of the car is somewhere in between.

You can call your local bank to get the book value of the car. It may be more difficult to obtain the wholesale value of the car because the amount of money a dealer is willing to pay for the car depends on the value of the new car that you are purchasing. You can determine the car's retail value by looking at comparable used car advertisements in the local newspaper or over the Internet.

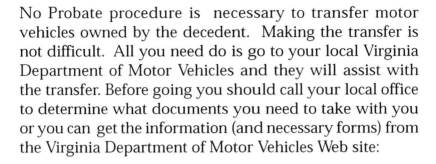

MAKING THE TRANSFER

No Probate procedure is necessary to transfer motor vehicles owned by the decedent. Making the transfer is not difficult. All you need do is go to your local Virginia Department of Motor Vehicles and they will assist with the transfer. Before going you should call your local office to determine what documents you need to take with you or you can get the information (and necessary forms) from the Virginia Department of Motor Vehicles Web site:

 DEPARTMENT OF MOTOR VEHICLES WEB SITE
http://www.dmv.state.va.us/

You need to transfer the car registration at the same time you transfer title to the car. If the car is to remain in Virginia, then the new owner needs to produce proof of insurance. If the car is going to be transferred out of state, then the Virginia registration needs to be cancelled.

TRANSFERRING THE MOBILE HOME

A mobile home is a motor vehicle, so the methods described can be used to transfer the decedent's mobile home. Before transferring the motor vehicle, you need to find out whether the land on which the mobile home is located was leased or owned by the decedent.

If the decedent was renting space in a trailer park, then you need to contact the trailer park owner to transfer the lease agreement to the beneficiary of the mobile home. If the decedent owned the land under the mobile home, then the land needs to be transferred to the proper beneficiary. See page 140 for information about transferring real property.

CLEARING THE DRIVER'S LICENSE RECORD

It is important to clear the decedent's driver's license or photo identification card record to prevent anyone from using the decedent's name for fraudulent purposes. You can clear the record at the same time you transfer the motor vehicle. If you are not transferring a car at this time you can clear the record by going to your local Department of Motor Vehicles Customer Service Center.

You will need to bring the following items with you:
- a certified copy of the death certificate
- the decedent's driver's license - or -
- the decedent's photo identification card record
- disabled parking placard (if any).

If you wish you can clear the record by sending a letter and a certified copy of the death certificate to:

Driver Licensing Division
Department of Motor Vehicles
P.O. Box 27412
Richmond, VA   23269

Ask that they clear the decedent's driving license and remove his name from the mailing list.

The leased car is not an asset of the estate because the decedent did not own the car. The leased car is a liability to the estate because the decedent was obligated to pay the balance of the monies owed on the lease agreement. The Personal Representative, or next of kin, needs to work out an agreement with the company to either assign the lease to a beneficiary or family member who will agree to pay for the lease or to have the estate pay off the lease by purchasing the car under the terms of the lease agreement.

Some lenders will allow the lease to be assigned to a beneficiary provided the estate remains liable for the balance of payment. In such cases, it is better to have the beneficiary refinance the car and have the original lease agreement paid in full.

If the remaining payments exceed the current market value of the car, there may be a temptation to hand the keys over to the leasing company. This may not be the best strategy, because the leasing company can sell the car and then sue the estate for the balance of the monies owed. If the decedent had no assets or if the only assets he had are creditor proof, then simply returning the car may be an option. But if the decedent's estate has assets available to pay the balance of the lease payments, then the Personal Representative needs to arrange to have the car transferred in a way that releases the estate from all further liability.

TRANSFERRING REAL PROPERTY

No Probate procedure is necessary to transfer Virginia real property if the decedent held the property:

⇨ as the owner of a life estate — or —

⇨ co-owner *with right of survivorship* — or —

⇨ as tenants by the entirety (i.e., as husband and wife)

The surviving party owns the property as of the decedent's date of death, but the decedent's name remains on the deed. The State Registrar of Vital Statistics keeps a record of the death, but the Registrar does not publish the death certificate so it is not part of the public record (VA 32.1-252). Anyone who examines title to the property will not know of the death unless a document is recorded in the county where the property is located. This is not a problem if you intend to sell or transfer the property. All you need do is produce a certified copy of the death certificate at closing.

If you do not intend to sell or transfer the property in the near future, then it is advisable to have documentation recorded showing that you are now the surviving owner. To do so, all you need do is go to the Clerk of the Circuit Court in the city or county where the property is located. The Clerk will give you an Affidavit to sign giving notice of the death.

Once signed, the Clerk will record the document and send an abstract of the Affidavit to the Commissioner of Revenue, who will then indicate the ownership of the property on the Land Books. Anyone who now examines the title to the property will know that the decedent no longer owns the property (VA 64.1-135).

Much the same procedure is followed for property held in the decedent's name only, or as a Tenant in Common. If the decedent died without a Will, then the decedent's Personal Representative needs to complete an Affidavit provided by the Clerk of the Circuit Court. The Affidavit will state the legal description of the property, and the names and last known addresses of the decedent's heirs. The Clerk will record the Affidavit and send an abstract of the Affidavit to the Commissioner of Revenue.

If no Probate procedure is necessary, the person who inherits the property can sign the Clerk's Affidavit, and have the property transferred. There is a Probate Tax on the property of 10 cents for every $100 of value that must be paid regardless of whether there is a Probate procedure (see Page 143) (VA 58.1-1713, 64.1-135).

No Affidavit is necessary if the decedent left a valid Will. Once the Will is admitted to Probate, the Clerk will give the Personal Representative a certified copy of the Will. The Personal Representative needs to have the certified copy of the Will recorded in each county where the decedent's real property is located (VA 55-6, 64.1-94).

If the decedent's Will was probated in another state, then a copy that is certified in the other state is not sufficient. The Clerk will require that the out of state Will be admitted to Probate in the county where the property is located. Once the Will is admitted to Probate in Virginia, the Clerk of the Probate Court will issue a certified copy of the Will that can be recorded in any Virginia county where real property owned by the decedent is located (VA 64.1-92).

You may save time if before going to the Circuit Court, you first call the Clerk. Some questions you might want answered are:

How do I get to the Court house?

What is the best time to meet with you?

What documents do I need to bring with me?

How much will it cost to record?

Is a personal check acceptable or do I need to bring cash or a money order?

The National Center For State Courts, located in Williamsburg, Virginia has a Web site that gives information about court systems for each state. You can find the address, phone number, and office hours of different city and county court houses. Some listings even contain pictures of the court house site.

WEB SITE FOR VIRGINIA STATE COURTS
http://www.ncsc.dni.us/

 CREDITORS HAVE RIGHTS

You may be thinking "This is easy. All I need do is go to the Clerk sign some papers, pay the tax and recording fee and the property is mine." But if there are any unpaid debts, you can be held responsible to pay those debts. And if the decedent died intestate and you are not the heir according to the Laws of Descent and Distribution, the proper heir has the right to sue you. It may cost you more to pay for your attorney fees than the property is worth. It might be better to go through a Probate procedure to be sure that no one has a prior claim to the property, and to be sure that no creditor can hold you responsible to pay the decedent's debt (VA 64.1-181, 64.1-183, 64.1-185).

THE FULL PROBATE PROCEDURE

There needs to be a full Probate administration if the decedent left personal property, in his name only, that is worth more than $10,000. The full Probate procedure is involved and time consuming; not to mention, expensive. Administration of the estate can take anywhere from several months to more than a year, depending on the size and complexity of the Estate. The procedure begins when someone is appointed as Personal Representative. But first the Probate Tax must be paid:

THE PROBATE ESTATE TAX

An estimated Probate Estate tax must be paid before anyone can be appointed as Personal Representative. The tax is 10 cents for each $100 of property transferred to a beneficiary either through the decedent's Will or through the Virginia Laws of Descent and Distribution. The tax applies to property located within Virginia. It does not apply to real property located in another state or country. And there is no Probate tax if the decedent's Probate Estate is $10,000 or less.

The tax is due and payable when property is being transferred regardless of whether there is actually a Probate procedure. As explained on page 141, it is possible to transfer real property without going through a Probate procedure, however the Probate Estate Tax needs to be paid before the property can be transferred. (VA 58.1-1712, 58.1-1713, 58.1-1715).

THE DUTIES OF PERSONAL REPRESENTATIVE

Settling a Probate Estate can be complex. The Personal Representative must take to take an inventory of all of the decedent's assets. He may need to employ an appraiser to determine the value of the property. The Personal Representative must identify the decedent's creditors and give them an opportunity to come forward and present their claims. Once the taxes, valid claims and expenses of the administration are paid, the Personal Representative will need to do an accounting, distribute the assets to the proper beneficiary and then close out the Probate estate.

All of the taxes, claims and expenses are paid from the Probate Estate and not from the Personal Representative's pocket; but if the Personal Representative makes a mistake, he may be made to pay for that mistake. He can be personally liable for property that is lost or damaged through his negligence. He can be liable if he does not perform his duties as required by law. For example, if he does not file tax returns correctly or on time, then he may be responsible to pay for fines levied against the estate because of his error (VA 26-5).

The Personal Representative needs to employ an attorney to guide him through the process. It then becomes the job of the attorney for the Personal Representative to see to it that the estate is administered properly and without any liability to the Personal Representative. The cost of employing an attorney is a proper charge to the Probate Estate.

YOUR RIGHTS AS A BENEFICIARY

As explained on page 91, the Commissioner of Accounts is in charge of supervising the administration, however, much of the Personal Representative's job is done independently and without seeking permission from the Probate Court. If you are a beneficiary of the decedent's estate, then it is important that you know what rights you have and how to assert those rights when necessary.

✧ RIGHT TO YOUR OWN ATTORNEY

The attorney who handles the estate is employed by, and represents, the Personal Representative. If the estate is sizeable, consider employing your own attorney to check that things are done properly and in a timely manner. Even with a small estate, you may want to consult with an attorney if at any time you are concerned about the way the Probate is being conducted.

✧ RIGHT TO APPROVE PERSONAL REPRESENTATIVE

Within 30 days of his appointment, the Personal Representative must write to the surviving spouse and all the beneficiaries, and give them his name, address, telephone number and the mailing address of the Clerk of the court where the Probate is being conducted (VA 64.1-122.2). If you have an objection to who is being appointed as Personal Representative, then this is the time to raise those objections to the Clerk. You can raise this, or any other objection you may have, without the assistance of an attorney, but it is best to consult with an attorney experienced in Probate matters before doing so. The attorney will be able to explain the proper procedure to raise the objection. More importantly, the attorney will be able to tell you which arguments have a good chance of succeeding and which may be doomed to failure and not worth pursuing.

✧ RIGHT TO DEMAND SUFFICIENT BOND

It doesn't happen often, but every now and again a Personal Representative will mismanage or run off with estate funds. A bond is insurance for the estate. If there is loss to the estate because of mismanagement of estate funds, the company that issued the bond will reimburse the estate for the loss.

The Clerk will require the Personal Representative to acquire a bond prior to issuing Letters, unless all of the beneficiaries are serving as Personal Representative. The value of the bond is based on the estimated value of the Probate Estate. If more assets are found, then you can ask that the bond be increased (VA 26-3, 64.1-119, 64.1-136).

The Clerk may decide not to require a bond if the Will specifically states that there be none. You can ask the Clerk to require a bond even though the Will says differently, if you are concerned about the safety of the estate funds (VA 64.1-121). An experienced Probate attorney can suggest to you a reasonable value to request for the bond after taking into consideration:

➪ the basic honesty and competency of the Personal Representative;

➪ whether the estate assets are easily transferable, such as cash and securities, or whether the Probate Estate is mostly real property, requiring Court authority to transfer;

➪ the cost of the bond (which ultimately is paid for by the beneficiaries of the estate).

✧ RIGHT TO A COPY OF THE WILL

The Personal Representative should, as a matter of courtesy, provide you with a copy of the Will. If he does not give you a copy, then once the Will has been admitted to Probate, you can obtain a copy from the Clerk of the Probate Court.

✧ RIGHT TO COPY OF INVENTORY

Within 4 months of his appointment, the Personal Representative must file an inventory of all of the property owned by the decedent. The inventory must including property that is not subject to Probate in Virginia, such as joint bank accounts or real property located in another state or country. The Personal Representative or his attorney should give you a copy of the inventory as soon as it is filed with the court (VA 26-12).

✧ RIGHT TO AN ACCOUNTING

The Personal Representative must file an accounting of all the estate property which he has received or disbursed within the first year of his appointment. He can file an earlier accounting at any time during the first year, but the initial accounting cannot be filed later than 16 months after his qualification. No accounting is required if all of the beneficiaries of the estate are also Personal Representatives of the estate (VA 26-17.5, 26-20.1).

You should receive a copy of the accounting as soon as it is filed. The accounting should start with the inventory value of the estate and end with the amount of money that will be left to distribute after all the bills have been paid. If the estate has significant assets you may want your own accountant to look over the final accounting and verify that it is correct.

✧ RIGHT TO COPY OF TAX RETURNS

Unless the decedent made other provisions, each person who inherits property needs to pay his/her share of state and federal taxes that may be due. This includes people who have inherited property without going through the Probate procedure. For example, if a beneficiary owned property jointly with right of survivorship, then the beneficiary is responsible to pay taxes that may be due on the share of the property inherited from the decedent.

Because each beneficiary may be personally liable to pay his/her share of the taxes, it is important that the beneficiary check to see that the proper tax returns are filed, and that all taxes paid. You can do this by asking the Personal Representative for copies of the returns and then checking the final accounting to be sure that any outstanding taxes were paid.

The Personal Representative is not required to give you a full copy of all returns, but under Virginia law, he must at least provide you with a copy of that portion of the tax return as it relates to the property that you inherit as a beneficiary of the estate (VA 64.1-161).

✧ RIGHT TO APPROVE FEES

The Personal Representative is entitled to a reasonable fee for administering the estate. It is not unusual for the Personal Representative to charge 5% of the value of the Probate estate for his services. If he is a beneficiary of the estate he may decide not to take a fee and just take his inheritance. The reason may be economic. Any fee the Personal Representative takes is taxable as ordinary income, but monies inherited are not taxable to him as a beneficiary. Ask the Personal Representative to tell you, in writing, whether he intends to ask for a fee, and if so, how much.

The Personal Representative has the right to employ an attorney to guide him through the procedure, and to have the attorney's fee paid with estate funds. You, as a beneficiary, have the right to know how much will be charged for his services. Ask the Personal Representative to give you a copy of the retainer agreement, so that you will know how much is being charged for legal fees. If the attorney is employed on an hourly basis, have the attorney give a written estimate of the time he expects to expend on the Probate procedure.

There is no statutory guideline for what is a "reasonable" fee for the attorney. You could call different law firms and ask what they charge to Probate an estate with similar assets, and that will give you some idea of the going rate. If after doing some "comparison shopping" you believe that either the Personal Representative's fee or his attorney's fee is not reasonable, you can negotiate with them to lower the fee. Whatever amount they charge must be approved by the Commissioner of Accounts, so if you cannot come to an agreement, you present your concerns to the Commissioner to consider (VA 26-30, 64.1-182).

✧   RIGHT TO RECEIVE A DEBT FREE INHERITANCE

Once a beneficiary finally receives his inheritance, the last thing he wants to hear is that there is some unfinished business, or worse yet that monies need to be paid from the inheritance he received. But that is just what could happen if the Personal Representative distributes the money before all the creditors are paid. Virginia law gives the decedent's creditors up to five years to sue any of the beneficiaries for monies owed.

You can protect yourself from this unhappy situation by checking to see that the Personal Representative gives proper notice to all of the decedent's known creditors, and then verifying that they were paid. Virginia law does not require that notice be published in the newspapers for unidentified creditors to come forward, unless someone asks the Court to order that it be done. Most Personal Representatives will ask the Court for such an order because it protects them from personal liability. You should verify that the Personal Representative intends to have notice published in the newspaper; and then have him provide you with a copy of the notice.

If the Personal Representative decides not to request publication, then you can do so. Once the Probate procedure begins, you can ask the Commissioner of Accounts to set a time and place for receiving proof of debts and demands for payment. If you make the request, then the Commissioner will publish notice in a newspaper at least 10 days before the hearing. You can make a second request for publication after the Personal Representative has filed his accounting. Upon your request, the Court will have notice published for 2 successive weeks. The notice will say that the estate is going to be distributed unless someone comes forward with an objection (VA 64.1-171, 64.1-179).

IT'S YOUR RIGHT - DON'T BE INTIMIDATED

As a beneficiary, you have many legal rights, but you may feel uncomfortable asserting those rights with a friend or family member who is Personal Representative. Don't be. It's your money and your legal right to be kept informed. Be especially firm if the Personal Representative waves you off with:

"You've known me for years. Surely you trust me."

People who are trustworthy, don't ask to be trusted. They do what is right. The very fact that the Personal Representative is resisting, is a red flag. In such situation, you can explain that it is not a matter of trust, but a matter of what is your legal right.

At the same time, keep things in perspective. Your relationship with the Personal Representative may be more important to you than the money you inherit. The job of settling an estate can be complex and demanding. If the Personal Representative is getting the job done, then let him know that you appreciate his efforts.

THE CHECK LIST

We discussed many things that need to be done when someone dies in the state of Virginia. The next page contains a check list that you may find helpful.

You can check those items that you need to do, and then cross them off the list once they are done. We made the list as comprehensive as possible, so many items may not apply in your case. In such case, you can cross them off the list or mark them *N/A* (not applicable).

Things to do

FUNERAL ARRANGEMENTS TO BE MADE

☐ AUTOPSY   ☐ ANATOMICAL GIFT
☐ DISPOSITION OF BODY OR ASHES

DEATH CERTIFICATE

GIVE COPY TO: _____

_____

_____

NOTICE OF DEATH

PEOPLE TO BE NOTIFIED _____

COMPANIES TO NOTIFY
☐ TELEPHONE COMPANY
     ☐ LOCAL CARRIER   ☐ LONG DISTANCE   ☐ CELLULAR
☐ NEWSPAPER (OBITUARY PRINTED)
☐ NEWSPAPER CANCELLED   ☐ deposit refund
☐ SOCIAL SECURITY
☐ INTERNET SERVER
☐ TELEVISION CABLE COMPANY
☐ POWER & LIGHT   ☐ deposit refund
☐ POST OFFICE
☐ OTHER UTILITIES (GAS, WATER)   ☐ deposit refund
☐ PENSION PLAN
☐ ANNUITY
☐ HEALTH INSURANCE COMPANY
☐ LIFE INSURANCE COMPANY
☐ HOME INSURANCE COMPANY
☐ MOTOR VEHICLE INSURANCE COMPANY
☐ CONDOMINIUM OR HOMEOWNER ASSOCIATION
☐ CANCEL SERVICE CONTRACT   ☐ deposit refund
☐ CREDIT CARD COMPANIES _____

     _____

     _____

Things to do

REMOVE DECEDENT AS BENEFICIARY OF:
- [ ] WILL   [ ] INSURANCE POLICY   [ ] PENSION PLAN
- [ ] BANK OR IRA ACCOUNT   [ ] SECURITY

DEBTS
PAY DECEDENT'S DEBTS (AMOUNT & CREDITOR)

_____

COLLECT MONIES OWED TO DECEDENT (AMOUNT & DEBTOR)

_____

TAXES
- [ ] FILE FINAL FEDERAL INCOME TAX RETURN
- [ ] FILE FINAL STATE INCOME TAX RETURN
- [ ] RECEIVE INCOME TAX REFUND
- [ ] FILE ESTATE TAX RETURN

PROPERTY TO BE TRANSFERRED
- [ ] PERSONAL EFFECTS
- [ ] MOTOR VEHICLE
- [ ] BANK ACCOUNT
- [ ] CREDIT UNION ACCOUNT
- [ ] IRA ACCOUNT
- [ ] SECURITIES
- [ ] BROKERAGE ACCOUNT
- [ ] INSURANCE PROCEEDS
- [ ] HOMESTEAD
- [ ] TIME SHARE
- [ ] OTHER REAL PROPERTY
- [ ] CONTENTS OF SAFE DEPOSIT BOX

OTHER THINGS TO DO

_____
_____
_____

Once the Probate procedure is over, you will be left with many documents and wonder which you need to keep:

COURT DOCUMENTS
You should keep a copy of the inventory to establish the value of property that you inherit. That value becomes your basis for any Capital Gains tax that you may need to pay in the future. Other than the inventory, there is no reason to keep any Court document, provided you are satisfied with the way things were done; and do not intend to take action against the Personal Representative, or his attorney. The Clerk of the Probate Court keeps the Probate file on record, so if for some reason you later need a copy of a Probate document, you can get it from the Clerk.

PERSONAL DOCUMENTS
You may wish to keep the decedent's personal papers (birth certificate, marriage certificate, naturalization papers, army records, religious documents, etc.) for your own personal records. You may want to keep the decedent's medical records in the event that a member of the family needs to check out a genetic disease.

TAX RECORDS
The IRS has up to three years to collect additional taxes, and you have up to 7 years to claim a loss from a worthless security, so you should keep the decedent's tax file for seven years from the date of filing the return. You can learn more about which records to keep from the IRS publication 552. You can get the publication by calling the IRS at (800) 829-3676 or you can download it from their Web site:

IRS WEB SITE
http://www.irs.gov

Preneed Arrangements   7

Death is a wake-up call because once someone close to us dies we are reminded of our own mortality. Many of us believe that death can be put off, but the inevitable is inevitable. Although we cannot change the fact of our death, we have the power to control the circumstances of our death by making preneed arrangements.

Preneed arrangements can be made so that you are buried in the manner you wish and where you wish. You can make arrangements that direct the kind of medical treatments you want to be given in the event you become seriously ill.

You can legally appoint someone to make your medical decisions in the event that you are too ill to speak for yourself. If you let that person know how you feel about life support systems, autopsies and anatomical gifts, then that person will be authorized to act on your behalf and see to it that your wishes are carried out.

As this chapter will show, it is relatively simple and inexpensive to make such preneed arrangements.

MAKING BURIAL ARRANGEMENTS

When making burial arrangements for the decedent, you may decide to purchase one or more burial spaces nearby for yourself or other family members.

If the decedent was buried in the family plot, then this is the time to take inventory of the number of spaces left and who in the family expects to use those spaces.

If all of the spaces are taken and if you plan to be cremated, then as explained in Chapter 1, some cemeteries will allow an urn to be placed in an occupied family plot. You can call the cemetery and ask them to explain their policy as it relates to the burial of an urn in a currently occupied grave site or mausoleum.

If this is not an option, and the cemetery of your choice has a columbarium, you might consider purchasing a space at this time.

If you wish to have your cremains scattered, then you need to let your next of kin know where and how this is to be done.

VETERAN OR
VETERAN'S SPOUSE

If you are an honorably discharged veteran, you have the right to be buried in a Veterans National Cemetery. You cannot reserve a grave site in advance. If your Veteran spouse was buried in a Veterans National Cemetery then you have the right to be buried in that same grave site unless soil conditions require a separate grave site.

If you wish to be buried in a Veterans National Cemetery, then check on current availability (see page 15 for telephone numbers). Let your next of kin know your choice of cemetery.

To establish your eligibility your next of kin will need to provide the following information:

➤ the veteran's rank, serial, Social Security and VA claim numbers

➤ the branch of service; the date and place of entry into and separation from the service

The next of kin will also need to provide the VA with a copy of the veteran's official military discharge document bearing an official seal or a DD 214 form.

If you wish to be buried in a national cemetery, then make all of these items readily accessible to your family.

MAKING FUNERAL ARRANGEMENTS

If you are financially able, in addition to purchasing a burial space, consider purchasing a Preneed funeral plan. It will be easier on your family emotionally and financially if you make your own funeral arrangements. If you do not have sufficient cash on hand for the kind of funeral you desire, then many funeral directors offer an installment payment plan.

Once you decide on a plan, the funeral director will present you with a contract. Virginia law 54.1-2820 requires that the seller use a form prepared by the Virginia Board of Funeral Directors and Embalmers. The form should contain the Board's address and telephone number.

Even though the seller gives you a standard form, it does not mean that it cannot be changed. If you are not satisfied with the way a certain section of the contract read, then attach an addendum to the contract that explains, in plain English, your understanding of that passage. If you are concerned about something that is not mentioned in the contract, then insist that the contract be amended to include that item.

In particular, check to see whether the contract answers the following questions.

Does the contract cover all costs?

The contract should contain an itemized list stating exactly what goods and services are included in the sales price. Ask the funeral director whether there will be any additional cost when you die. For example, if you have not purchased a burial space, then that cost needs to be factored in. If you made provision for a burial space, then you need to let the funeral director know where you have arranged to be buried. If you have not made such provision, then the funeral director can assist you in making burial arrangements.

Is the price guaranteed?

Some Preneed plans have a fixed price for the goods and services you chose. Such contracts guaranteed that the goods and services purchased or items of the same style and quality will be provided upon your death, regardless of when you die. You need to check out whether the person who is selling you the Contract is the one who is going to provide the goods and services that you are purchasing. If not, then Virginia law requires that the seller of the contract must attach his agreement with the company that is actually going to provide the goods and services to your contract (VA 54.1-2820 (A) 10). You may want to read such an agreement to be sure that the provider has agreed to honor your contract.

If the price for the goods and services that you have chosen under the Preneed Funeral Contract is not fixed, then the company can charge additional monies upon your death. In these days of an ever increasing life expectancy, it is important that such a contract clearly state how the price will be determined when the contract is finally put into effect.

How are your contract funds protected?
You can fund your plan by purchasing a life insurance policy. Virginia law requires that the face value of the policy be adjusted each year in accordance with the U.S. Consumer Price Index, or, the monies payable at death must equal the amount of monies paid for the policy, plus interest. For the first 15 years the interest must be at least 5% compounded annually. The law also requires that the relationship between the seller of the contract, the company that is going to provide the goods and services, and the insurance company be made known to you (VA 54.1-2820 B). If they are all one and the same, you may want to consider purchasing an insurance policy from an independent insurance company.

You may decide to pay cash for your Preneed Funeral Plan. In that case Virginia law requires that the funds be placed in a Trust account in a bank in the Commonwealth of Virginia. If you have a guaranteed price contract, then 90% of the monies paid must be placed in the Trust account. If you do not have a fixed priced contract, then 100% of the monies you pay must be placed in the Trust account. The funds must be deposited within 30 days. You may want to have your contract state that you will be provided with proof of deposit.

Virginia law gives you the right to choose the Trustee of the account. The law allows the funeral home to serve as Trustee, provided the funds cannot be removed unless there are least two different Trustees who must act jointly to remove the funds (VA 54.1-2822).

Is the funeral firm reputable?

All these precautions don't do much good if you are not dealing with a reputable company. It is important to take the time to check up on whoever is selling you the contract. In Virginia, anyone who offers Preneed Funeral contracts to the public must be licensed to do so. You can check to see if the seller is licensed by calling the Board of Funeral Directors and Embalmers at (800) 533-1560. Out of state call (804) 662-9907. You may also want to ask how long they have been in business and whether any complaints have been filed against them.

Can you cancel the contract?

Virginia law gives you the right to cancel your Preneed Funeral Contract at any time. If you revoke the contract within 30 days of signing the contract then you have the right to receive all of you monies back, plus interest, if the monies were placed in a Trust account. After 30 days the amount you will receive back depends on the terms of the contract. Virginia law requires that you receive all of the monies in the Trust account, but in a guaranteed price contract, only 90% of the funds are deposited, so at the very least you will forfeit 10% of what you paid.

It is important to read and understand that part of the contract that deals with your right to revoke the contract and get your money back. If you are using an insurance policy to fund the plan, then you need to know how much you will lose should you cancel the insurance policy. If you intend to pay for your Preneed Funeral Contract on an installment basis, then you need to know how much of the monies you pay will be returned to you in the event that you default on payment.

FUNERAL PLANS FOR THOSE ON PUBLIC ASSISTANCE

People who are applying for, or receiving, Medicaid, Supplemental Security Income ("SSI") or other public assistance program have limits on the amount of assets that they own. If someone purchases a Preneed Funeral Plan, then the monies paid into the plan count as an asset because the purchaser of the plan can revoke the contract and get his money back. Understanding the problem, Virginia law allows the applicant to pay for a plan by setting up a Trust. The Trust must be set up in accordance with Virginia statute (VA 54.1-2820 (A7), 55-19.5). You will need an experienced Elder Law attorney to prepare the Trust in conformity with the law.

If you are in the process of applying for a public assistance program, then before finalizing your funeral plan, it is prudent to check with your local Department of Medical Assistance Services to be sure that your plan will not affect your ability to qualify for the program.

Even if you are in good health at this time, it is a good idea to have your contract provide that you can change your plan to conform to state and federal law, if at any time you need to apply for a public assistance program.

Suppose you die in another state or country?

Your contract should spell out what provision will be made in the event that you move to another state or die in another state or country. Many funeral firms are part of a national funeral service corporation with funeral firms located throughout the United States. You may be able to have the contract provide that there will be no additional charge if the contract is performed by one of the funeral firms owned by the parent company.

Can the plan be changed after your death?
It may happen that your heirs need to cancel the plan after your death because:

➤ your body is missing or cannot be recovered, or

➤ you were buried by another funeral home because no one knew that you had a Preneed contract, or

➤ you died in another country and were buried there.

Or perhaps your heirs decide on a plan different than the one you purchased. Funeral firms generally allow heirs to make changes to the plan you paid for such as:

➤ purchasing a more expensive plan and paying the difference

➤ changing to a lesser plan and receiving a refund.

You need to check to see that your contract addresses these issues.

You may wonder why anyone would think of changing the decedent's funeral plan, but consider that in today's market, it is not uncommon for a Preneed contract to cost several thousand dollars. A top end funeral complete with solid bronze casket can cost upwards of $40,000.

And there may be other motivations. Consider the case of Mona, a difficult woman with a personality that can only be described as "sour." Her husband deserted her after four years of marriage leaving her to raise their son, Lester, by herself. Once Lester was grown, Mona made it clear to him that she had done her job and now he was on his own. Lester could have used some help. He married and had three children. One of his children suffered with asthma and it was a constant struggle to keep up with the medical bills.

Mona believed in being good to herself. She did not intend to, nor did she, leave much money when she died. She knew that Lester would not be able to afford a "proper" burial for her, so she purchased a funeral plan and paid close to $18,000 for it. She was pleased when the funeral director told her that the monies would be kept safely in a Trust account until the time they were needed.

Lester was not familiar with Virginia law, so when Mona died he asked an attorney at the Legal Aid office to determine whether the Preneed contract was revocable.

It was.

You know the ending to this story.

If you are concerned that you get the exact type of funeral that you want, with no changes, then your attorney can suggest any number of ways to do so. The simplest way may be to make the Preneed funeral contract irrevocable by saying that no changes can be made to the contract, and having the monies placed in an Irrevocable Trust. You may also want to appoint someone to be your Health Care Agent to see that your funeral is conducted in the manner you wish. See page 168 for a discussion of how to appoint a Health Care Agent.

You may be thinking "Revocable. Irrevocable. All this contract stuff is giving me a headache. Why can't I just set aside some money and let my kids figure it out?"

The problem with that approach is that the cost of your final days may leave you with little or no funds for your burial. To avoid the problem, you could purchase a life insurance policy to fund your funeral and burial, naming one or two trusted family members as the beneficiary of the policy. It is important that the person who is to receive the insurance funds clearly understands why he/she is named as beneficiary of the policy. It is equally important that the beneficiary agree to use the monies for the intended purpose.

It isn't so much that a family member is not trustworthy as it is that they may not understand what you intended — especially in those cases where other funds are available to pay for the funeral. Too often insurance funds are left to a sibling who then refuses to contribute to the cost of the funeral saying in effect "Dad wanted me to have this money — that's why he left it to me."

To avoid a misunderstanding, put it in writing. It need not be a formal contract. It could be something as simple as a letter to the insurance beneficiary, with copies to your next of kin. The next page contains a sample letter.

Dear Romita,

I purchased a $20,000 insurance policy today naming you as beneficiary of the policy. As we discussed this money is to be used to pay for the following:
- my funeral and grave site
- my headstone
- perpetual care for my grave
- airfare for each of my grandchildren to attend the funeral
- dinner for the family after the wake
- lunch for the family after the funeral

If there is any money left over, please accept it as my thanks for all the effort spent on my behalf.

Love,
Dad

P.S. I am sending a copy of this letter to your brother so that he will know that all arrangements have been made.

Whether or not you arrange to pay for your burial or funeral, you need to let your next of kin know your feelings about the burial procedure. Let your family know whether you wish to be cremated or buried. If you wish to have a religious service, then let your family know the type of service and where it is to be held. Let the family know where you wish to be buried, or if you intend to be cremated, then where to place the ashes.

ANATOMICAL GIFTS

If you want to make an anatomical gift to take effect upon your death, you can make the gift as part of your Will; but it may be some time before your Will is located. The better route is to make the donation by a separate writing. You can complete a organ donor card when you apply for your Virginia driver's license or Virginia Photo Identification Card.

If you do not want the fact that you are an organ donor indicated on your driver's licence or Photo ID, you can sign a donor card and give it to a trusted family member. Virginia statute 54.1-2984 contains a form that you can complete to make the donation. You can download the statute from the Virginia statute Web site:

VIRGINIA STATUTE WEB SITE
http://www.state.va.us

If you are advanced in years, your local Organ Procurement Organization will probably not consider your body for transplantation of body parts, but you can still donate your body for education and research. If you wish to make such as donation you can call the Virginia State Anatomical Program (804) 786-2479 and they will send you information about making the donation.

If you do not wish to make an anatomical gift, then let your family know how you feel.

AUTOPSIES

As discussed in Chapter 1, some autopsies are optional. If you have strong feelings about allowing an optional autopsy or not allowing the procedure, then let your family know how you feel.

Of course, there are problems with just telling someone how you feel about your burial arrangements, autopsies, and anatomical gifts:

THE PERSON DOES NOT CARRY OUT YOUR WISHES

Without written instructions, your next of kin will decide and then authorize the disposition of your remains. Whether they authorize an anatomical gift or an autopsy may depend more about how they feel about the procedure than what you wish.

Sometimes the person you tell may not understand what you said or perhaps they hear only what they want to hear. An example that comes to mind is the mother who complained that she felt like a burden to her children. She would often say "When I die, burn my body and throw my ashes out to sea." Her children paid no attention. No one asked, nor did they even think about, what she really wanted. When she died she was given a full funeral and buried in a local cemetery.

Even if you tell someone and trust that person to carry out your wishes, it could be that the person you confide in cannot carry out your instructions. For example, if you tell your spouse what arrangements to make, then he/she may become incapacitated or die before you do; or perhaps you both die together in a natural disaster or in a plane crash.

YOU TELL THE WRONG PERSON

You may tell someone who does not have authority to carry out your wishes. That was the case with James. Once his wife died, he moved to a retirement community where he lived for 15 years until his death. James had two sons who lived in different states. Although he loved his sons, he had difficulty talking to either of them about serious matters. It was easier for him to talk with his friends in the retirement community. They often spoke about dying and how they felt about different burial arrangements. James would reminisce about his youth and growing up in a farming community in the plains state of Kansas. "I was happy and free. Out there you had room to breathe. It would be nice to be buried there — peaceful and spacious."

When he died, his friends told his sons about their father's desire to be buried in Kansas. They met the suggestion with scepticism and pragmatism:

"Dad didn't say anything like that to me."

"It would cost us double, if we had to arrange for burial in another state. I'm sure he didn't have that kind of expense in mind."

WHO WANTS TO TALK ABOUT IT?

For many people the main problem with telling someone what to do when you die is talking about your death. It may be an uncomfortable, if not unpleasant, subject for you to bring up, and for your family to discuss. If this is the case, then consider putting the information in writing and give the instructions to the person who will have the job of carrying out your wishes.

APPOINTING A HEALTH CARE AGENT

You can legally appoint someone to carry out your wishes relating to the care of your person, by signing a document called an *Advance Medical Directive*. Virginia statute 54.1-2984 contains a statutory form that you can use to appoint a *Health Care Agent* to make your medical decisions in the event that you are too ill to do so yourself.

The statutory form contains a *Living Will* that tells your Health Care Agent whether you do (or do not) want life support systems to be used in the event that you are dying and there is no hope for your recovery. If you want to make an anatomical gift, then you can give your Health Care Agent authority to consent to the gift on your behalf (see page 5). If you do not wish to make an anatomical gift, then you can direct your Health Care Agent to not allow the procedure.

You can prepare your own Advance Medical Directive by copying the statutory form of the Advance Medical Directive. You can look up the statute by going to the nearest courthouse law library. You can also download the form from the Internet:

 VIRGINIA STATUTE WEB SITE
http://www.state.va.us

You can have your attorney prepare an Advance Medical Directive especially designed to meet your special needs. For example, you can include funeral or burial arrangements as part of your Medical Directive (VA 54.1-2825). It makes more sense to put these instructions in your Medical Directive rather than in your Will. Your Will may not be found for several days after your death, but your Advance Medical Directive is available to your Health Care Agent as soon as it is signed.

If you do not appoint someone to act as your Health Care Agent and you are too sick to make your own medical decisions, then the person with priority to make your medical decisions is established by Virginia statute:

1st   court appointed guardian (if any); or
2nd   spouse; or
3rd   adult child; or
4th   parent of patient; or
5th   adult brother or sister; or
6th   any other relative in the descending order of blood relationship

(VA 54.1-2986).

A person with priority must be reasonably available, willing and competent to make medical decisions for you. If not, the next one with priority will make the decision. If there are several people with equal authority and they disagree about the proposed treatment, the statute authorizes the doctor to follow the direction of a majority.

If this order of priority is not as you wish, or if there is someone you wish to exclude altogether from making your health care decisions, then it is important to sign an Advance Medical Directive and appoint the person of your choice to act as your Health Care Surrogate. If not, life decisions made for you, may not be as you would have wished.

George is a case in point. His wife suffered from Alzheimer's disease. He cared for her at home for as long as he was able, but finally, it was too much for him and he placed her in a local nursing facility. He and his two daughters visited her frequently, even though she scarcely recognized them.

Emily's husband also suffered from Alzheimer's disease and was at the same facility. George and Emily met at the nursing home support group and found that they had much in common. After visiting with their respective spouses they would go to the local coffee shop. One thing led to another, and soon they were an item.

George's daughters were not happy with the coupling. They criticized everything about Emily, from the way she dressed to her table manners. When Emily moved in with George, his daughters made cutting remarks about Emily's moral character. Emily didn't take it personally. She believed the girls were more concerned about their inheritance than George's happiness. A second marriage might cut into what they already considered to be rightfully theirs.

Not that George and Emily planned to wed. They both loved their respective spouses and had no intention of trying to obtain a divorce. Their understanding was that if and when they both were single, they would discuss marriage at that time.

Meanwhile, George and Emily enjoyed each other, feeling and acting like a couple of teenagers. But their happiness lasted only a few months. George suffered a stroke while driving a car. His injuries from the accident combined with the severity of the stroke made for a bleak prognosis. The doctors said George would die unless they put him on a ventilator and inserted a feeding tube. Even with life support systems, it was not expected that he would ever come out of the coma.

Emily pleaded to keep him alive. "Let's try everything. If he doesn't improve we can always discontinue the life support systems later."

George's daughters did not see it that way. "Why torture him with needles and tubes? Let him pass on peacefully."

George never signed a Living Will so no one knew whether he would want life support systems to be applied. He never appointed anyone to be his Health Care Agent to make his health care decisions in the event he was unable to do so. In the absence of an Advance Medical Directive, the doctors had no choice. Under Virginia law, the daughters were 3rd in priority. Emily was not a member of the family, so she had no priority at all.

George died.

Everyman's Estate Plan

The first six chapters of this book describe how to wind up the affairs of the decedent. As you read those chapters, you learned about the kinds of problems that can occur when settling the decedent's Estate. It is relatively simple for you to set up an Estate Plan so that your family members are not burdened with similar problems. An **Estate Plan** is the arranging of one's finances to reduce (if not eliminate) Probate costs and Estate taxes, and to ensure that your property is transferred quickly and at little cost.

If you think that only wealthy people need to prepare an Estate Plan, you are mistaken. Each year, heirs of relatively modest estates, spend thousands of dollars to settle an Estate. A bit of planning could have eliminated most, if not all, of the expense and hassle suffered by those families.

The suggestions in this chapter are designed to assist the average person in preparing a practical and inexpensive Estate Plan, so we named this chapter EVERYMAN'S ESTATE PLAN.

Once you create your own Estate Plan, you can be assured that your family will not be left with more problems than happy memories of you.

AVOIDING PROBATE

TRUE OR FALSE?

( ) If you have a Will, then there will need
to be a Probate administration.

( ) Probate is only necessary if you don't have a Will.

( ) Probate is necessary if you leave anything worth
more than $10,000.

If you answered false to all of the, then you are either a lawyer or you carefully read chapters 5 and 6.

For those who do not enjoy "Pop Quizzes," please forgive our reversion to educator (or maybe pedant). The point we were attempting to make is that:

> Whether a Probate procedure is necessary has nothing to do with whether there is a Will, or even how much money is involved. The determining factor is how the property is titled (owned).

There are three ways to title property:

✧ jointly with another
✧ in trust for another
✧ in your name only.

In general, property held jointly or in trust for someone goes directly to the intended beneficiary without the need for Probate. There may need to be a Probate procedure if property is held in the decedent's name only.

In this chapter we explore the pros and cons of titling property in each of the three ways, beginning with holding property jointly with another.

OWNERSHIP OF BANK ACCOUNTS

You can arrange to have all of your bank accounts set up so that should you die, the money goes directly to a beneficiary. For example, suppose all you own is a bank account and you want whatever you have in this account to go to your son and daughter when you die. You might think that a simple solution is to put each child's name on the account, but first consider the problems associated with a joint account:

⊠ POTENTIAL LIABILITY

If you hold a bank account jointly with your adult child and that child is sued or gets a divorce then the child may need to disclose his ownership of the joint account. In such a case, you may find yourself spending money to prove that the account was established for convenience only and that all of the money in that account really belongs to you.

⊠ OVERREACHING

If you set up a joint account with your child so that the child has authority to withdraw funds from the account, then funds may be withdrawn without your authorization. If you open a joint account with two of your children, then after your death the first child to the bank may decide to withdraw all of the money and that will, at the very least, cause hard feelings between them.

⊠ THE MINOR CHILD

In Virginia, a minor can own a savings or checking account alone or jointly with another. A minor can lease a safe deposit box in his name only or jointly with another (VA 6.1-194.55). But if you make a minor the joint owner of your account, would you want the child to be able to remove money from your account? Would you want the minor to be able to go to the bank and withdraw everything in your safe deposit box?

Because of these inherent problems, you might want to hold the funds so that your beneficiary does not gain access to the monies until and unless you die. There are three ways to do so: the "in trust for" account, the "pay on death" bank account and the "transfer on death" securities registration.

THE IN TRUST FOR ("ITF") ACCOUNT

You can direct a financial institution to hold your account *In Trust For* ("ITF") one or more beneficiaries that you name. Your contract with the bank will state that the beneficiary does not have access to the account until and unless you die (VA 6.1-125.1).

THE PAY ON DEATH ("POD") ACCOUNT

You can have a contract with the bank that directs the bank to *Pay On Death* ("POD") all of the money in the account to one or more beneficiaries that you name.

With both the ITF and POD account:

⇨ During his lifetime the owner of the account is free to change beneficiaries without asking the beneficiary's permission to do so.

⇨ The beneficiary does not have access to the account until the owner of the account dies.

Once the owner of the account dies, the beneficiary can take possession of the account, but if the decedent's Personal Representative needs money to pay for the decedent's debts, he can ask the beneficiary to return as much money from the account as needed to pay the debt. There is a two year statute of limitations, so if monies are needed from the account, the request must be made within two years from the date of death (VA 6.1-125.8, 6.1-125.11)

You can open an account with PAY ON DEATH instructions to give the money to your child when you die, and if the child dies before you, then to your grandchildren in equal shares. For example:

Eldon Connors POD Betty Connors LDPS

which is short-hand for:

"ELDON CONNORS is the owner of the account. On his death, pay the money in the account to BETTY CONNORS, but if she dies first, then give it to her lineal descendants, in equal shares, per stirpes" (VA 64.1-206.8).

There may be times when you wish to hold an account jointly (say with your spouse) and have your children inherit the money when you both die. For example:

ELDON CONNORS and LORRAINE CONNORS,
JOINT ACCOUNT WITH SURVIVORSHIP, POD
ELDON CONNORS, JR. AND FRED CONNORS,

⇨ The children (Eldon, Jr. and Fred) have no right to the account during the lifetime of their parents.

⇨ If either Eldon or Lorraine dies, then the surviving party owns the account, and is free to close the account or change the beneficiary of the account.

⇨ Once Eldon and Lorraine are deceased, their sons share the money in the account equally.

⇨ If one of the children dies before the parent dies, then the remaining son gets all of the money in the account (VA 6.1-125.5).

THE TRANSFER ON DEATH REGISTRATION

The Virginia law for securities is similar to the statute for bank accounts in that you can arrange to have a security (a stock, bond or securities account) transferred to a beneficiary upon your death. You can instruct the holder of the security to **Transfer On Death** ("TOD") to a named beneficiary. As with the POD designation, the TOD registration has no effect on the ownership of the security until the owner of the security dies. For example:

TANYA BEDDIE TOD LUCINDA BEDDIE

Once Tanya dies, all Lucinda need do is produce a certified copy of the death certificate and the security will be transferred to Lucinda. Should Lucinda die before Tanya, then the security will become part of Tanya's Estate (VA 64.1-206.4).

If the owners of the security wish to have someone inherit the property when they both die, then Virginia law requires that they hold the security as joint tenants with rights of survivorship; i.e., the beneficiary cannot inherit the security until they both die. The security can be titled as:

TIM REILLY and OLIVIA REILLY, JOINT TENANTS
WITH SURVIVORSHIP TOD STUART REILLY

Should both parents die, Stuart will inherit the security. If Stuart dies before his parents, then the security will go to the Estate of the last parent to die (VA 64.1-206.2, 64.1-206.5).

If your Estate consists only of bank accounts and/or securities, and you want all of your property to go to one or two beneficiaries without the need for Probate, but with maximum control and protection of your funds during your lifetime, then holding your property in any of these beneficiary forms:

"In Trust For" "Pay-On-Death" "Transfer-On-Death" should accomplish your goal.

GIFT TO MINOR

At the beginning of this chapter, we identified three problems with a joint account: potential liability if the joint owner is sued; overreaching by the joint owner, and holding an account jointly with a minor. The ITF, POD and TOD account each solve the problem of potential liability and overreaching, but if the beneficiary of such account is a minor, there still is the problem of the a child having access to a large sum of money.

The company in possession of the funds may decide to deposit the funds with the Clerk of the Circuit Court. If the account is $10,000 or less, the Judge will probably distribute the funds to the child's parent or guardian. For accounts over $10,000, the court may decide that it is necessary to appoint a Conservator of the child's Estate (VA 8.01-606).

This presents two problems. If the Court decides to have the parent take possession of the funds, then the parent can spend the money for the minor as he/she sees fit. The child may never even know of your gift. You may be thinking that it might be best that the child inherits more than $10,000, this way a Court will see to it that the monies are held safely till the child reaches 18. But that only presents a new set problems. It takes time, effort and money to set up a conservatorship. If you leave the child a significant amount of money, then the Conservator has the right to charge to manage those funds. It could happen that the cost of the conservatorship significantly reduces the amount of money inherited by the child.

There are ways to avoid the problem of having a Conservator appointed to care for property inherited by a child, and yet ensuring that the monies are protected. We will discuss those methods, in detail, at the beginning of the next chapter.

THE GIFT OF REAL PROPERTY

As explained in Chapter 5, if you own real property together with another, then who will own the property upon your death depends on how the Grantee is identified on the face of the deed. If you compare the Grantee clause of the deed to the examples on pages 101 through 104 you can determine who will inherit that property should you die. If you are not satisfied with the way the property will be inherited, then you need to consult with an attorney to change the deed so that it will conform to your wishes.

If you own the property in your name only, then once you die, your beneficiary might be able to transfer the property without any need for Probate (see page 141). Virginia is unique in that you may be able to transfer real property without going through a full Probate procedure, but if you have more than $10,000 in personal property, then Probate is necessary. Many states are just the opposite. They have relatively simple procedures for transferring personal property, but require a full Probate procedure for the transfer of real property.

OUT OF STATE PROPERTY
If you have out-of-state property, then it is important to find out what is necessary to transfer that property in the event of your death. If you want to avoid Probate in that state, then consider having the deed changed so that you and a beneficiary are joint owners with rights of survivorship. If you do so then should either of you die, the other will own the property 100%. You might also think about transferring the property to your beneficiary and keeping a Life Estate for yourself.

Of course there is a downside. You will not be able to sell that property during your lifetime without the beneficiary's permission. And if the beneficiary gives permission and the property is sold, the beneficiary will have the legal right to a part of the proceeds of the sale. There are also tax consequences to consider, because when you make the transfer, you are in effect, making a gift.

TAX CONCERNS FOR REAL PROPERTY TRANSFERS

⊠ POSSIBLE GIFT TAX

If the value of the transfer is worth more than $10,000 you need to file a gift tax return. For most of us, this is not a problem because no gift tax need be paid unless the value of the property (plus the value of all gifts in excess of $10,000 per person, per year, that you gave over your lifetime) exceeds the current Gift Tax exclusion value (see Page 37). If your Estate is in that tax bracket, then you need to be aware that you are "using up" your tax exclusion.

⊠ POSSIBLE CAPITAL GAINS TAX

If you gift the property to the child, when he sells the property he will be subject to a Capital Gains Tax on the increase in value from the price you paid to the selling price at the time of the sale. If you do not make the gift during your lifetime, the child will inherit the property with a step-up in basis, i.e., he will inherit the property at its market value as of the date of death. Under today's tax structure and continuing until 2009, that step-up in basis is unlimited. If your child sells the property when it is inherited, no Capital Gains Tax is due regardless of how large the step-up in basis. In 2010, there will be a limit on amount that can be inherited free of the Capital Gains Tax but that limit is quite high so for most of us this is not a concern (see Page 36).

CAUTION   GIFT OF HOMESTEAD

Some elderly parents are concerned that they may need nursing care at some time in the future and lose all of their life savings to pay for that care. More than the fear of their own impoverishment, is the fear of the loss of their child's inheritance. Most parents want to have their children inherit the one thing the parent has of value, namely their homestead. Some may think the safest way to avoid the loss of their homestead in their later years is to transfer the homestead to their child with the understanding that the parents will continue to live there until they die. Should you do so, then you risking the unfavorable tax consequences discussed on the last page, and three other risks:

⊠ RISK OF LOSS

If you transfer real property to your child it could be lost if the child runs into serious financial difficulties or gets sued. This is especially a risk if your child is a professional (doctor, nurse, accountant, financial planner, attorney, etc.). If your child is found to be personally liable for the damage, then your homestead could become part of the settlement of that law suit.

If your child is (or gets) married, then this complicates matters even more so. If the child is divorced, the property will need to be included as part of the settlement agreement. This may be to your child's detriment because the child may need to share the value of the property with his/her ex-spouse. If you do not transfer the property, then it cannot become part of the marital equation.

⊠ LOSS OF HOMESTEAD CREDITOR PROTECTION

Virginia law allows up to $5,000 of your real or personal property to be exempt from your creditors. If you have dependents, then you are allowed an additional $500 per dependent. If you are a Veteran with a disability of 40% or more, then you get to keep an additional $2,000. Should a creditor force the sale of your homestead, then you get to keep at least $5,000 of the value of your home. The only exception is monies owed on a mortgage, or for back support obligations (VA 34-4, 34-4.1, 34-5).

And a transfer of your homestead to a child is a double loss of the homestead creditor protection. If the child does not occupy that property as his homestead, then there is no homestead creditor protection whatsoever. The child's creditors can force the sale of the property (that's your home) for relatively small amounts of unpaid debts.

⊠ POSSIBLE LOSS OF GOVERNMENT BENEFITS

If you transfer property, then depending upon the value of the transfer, you could be disqualified from receiving Medicaid or Supplemental Security Income ("SSI") benefits for up to 3 years from the date of transfer to a person; and up to 5 years if you transfer the property to an irrevocable Trust. It could well happen that you might need extended nursing care during that penalty period.

If you are considering transferring your homestead because of the your concern for the cost of future health care, then before doing so, consult with an Elder Law attorney. He will be able to offer you several ways to protect your assets, and still ensure that you receive the health care that you may require in your later years.

 **LAWYER**   OUT OF STATE PROPERTY

Each state is in charge of the way property located in that state is transferred. If you own property in another state (or country) then you need to consult with an attorney in that state (or country) to determine how that property will be transferred to your beneficiaries once you die. Most state laws are similar to Virginia, namely, property held as **JOINT TENANTS WITH RIGHTS OF SURVIVORSHIP** or a **LIFE ESTATE INTEREST** are transferred without the need for Probate.

If you own property in another state in your name only, or as a **TENANT IN COMMON,** or if you hold property with your spouse in a community property state, then a Probate procedure may need to be held in that state. If it is necessary to have a Probate procedure in Virginia, then an ancillary (secondary) procedure will need to be held in the state where the property is located. This could have the effect of doubling the cost of Probate.

Still another problem is the matter of taxes. Some states have an inheritance or transfer tax. Estate taxes may be due in the state where the property as well as in Virginia. It may be necessary to file a tax return in two states. In addition to increased taxes, this can double the cost of the accounting fees.

You may wish to consult with an attorney for suggestions about how to set up your Estate Plan to avoid such problems.

A TRUST MAY BE THE SOLUTION (OR NOT)

A full Probate procedure may be necessary if you hold personal property in your name only that is worth more than $15,000, or if you hold real property as a Tenant-In-Common or in your name only. We explored different ways to re-title property to avoid Probate, but these methods may have trade-offs that are unacceptable to you. One way to avoid many of these potential problems is to set up a *Revocable Living Trust* (also known as an *Inter Vivos Trust*).

A Revocable Living Trust is designed to care for your property during your lifetime and then to distribute your property once you die without the need for Probate. You may have been encouraged to set up such a Trust by your financial planner, or attorney, or accountant. Even people of modest means are being encouraged to use a Trust as the basis of their Estate Plan. But Trusts also have their pros and cons. Before getting into that, let's first discuss what a Trust is and how it works:

SETTING UP A TRUST

To create a Trust, an attorney prepares the Trust document in accordance with the client's needs and desires. The person who signs the document is called the *Trustor* or *Settlor.* If the *Trustor* also funds the Trust, then he is also referred to as the *Grantor.* We will refer to the Revocable Living Trust as the "Living Trust" or just the "Trust" and the person setting up the Trust as the "Grantor." The Trust document identifies who is to be the Trustee (manager) of property placed in the Trust. Usually the Grantor appoints himself as Trustee so that he is in total control of property that he places into the Trust. The Trust document also names a Successor Trustee who will take over the management of the Trust property should the Trustee resign, or become disabled or die.

Once the Trust document is properly signed, the Grantor transfers property into the Trust. The Grantor does this by changing the name on the account from his individual name to his name as Trustee. For example, if Elaine Richards sets up a Trust naming herself as Trustee, and she wishes to place her bank account into the Trust then all she need do is instruct the bank to change the name on the account from ELAINE RICHARDS to:

ELAINE RICHARDS, TRUSTEE of the ELAINE RICHARDS REVOCABLE TRUST AGREEMENT DATED JULY 12, 2001.

When the change is made, all the money in the account becomes Trust property. Elaine (wearing her Trustee hat) has total control of the account, taking money out, and putting money in, as she sees fit. Similarly, if she wants to put real property into the Trust all she need do is have her attorney prepare a new deed with the Grantee identified as ELAINE RICHARDS, TRUSTEE (see page 105 for an example of real property placed into a Trust).

The Trust document states how the Trust property is to be managed during Elaine's lifetime. Should Elaine become disabled the Trust will provide for her Successor Trustee to take over and manage the Trust property. Because the Trust is revocable, if she wishes, Elaine can terminate the Trust at any time and have the Trust property placed back into her own individual name. If she does not revoke her Trust during her lifetime, then once she dies the Trust becomes irrevocable, and her Successor Trustee must follow the terms of the Trust Agreement as it is written. If the Trust says to give the Trust property to certain beneficiaries, then the Successor Trustee will do so; and in most cases without any Probate procedure. If the Trust directs the Successor Trustee to continue to hold property in Trust and use the money to take care of a member of Elaine's family, then the Successor Trustee will do so.

THE GOOD PART

Setting up a Trust has many good features.

☆☆ AVOID PROBATE

In Virginia, Probate can be time consuming and very expensive. Both the Personal Representative and his attorney are entitled to payment for their services. These fees can be significant. It may be necessary to hire accountants and appraisers, as well. If you have property in two states, then two Probate procedures may be necessary (one in each state) and that could have the effect of doubling the cost of Probate. If the Trust is properly drafted and your property placed into the Trust, you should be able to avoid Probate altogether.

☆ CARE FOR FAMILY MEMBER:

You can make provision in your Trust to care for a minor child or family member after you die. If your family member is immature or a born spender, you can set up a Spendthrift Trust to protect him/her from squandering his inheritance. You can direct your Successor Trustee to use Trust funds to pay for the family member's health care, education or living expenses, and nothing more. The Trust funds can be protected from the beneficiary's creditors, but only to a maximum of one million dollars. Virginia law makes anything over one million dollars available to pay for the beneficiary's debts (VA 55-19).

☆ AVOID APPOINTMENT OF A CONSERVATOR

Once you have a Trust you do not need to worry about who takes care of your property should you become disabled or too aged to handle your finances. The person you appointed as Successor Trustee will take over the care of the Trust property if you are unable to do so. If you do not have a Trust and you become incapacitated, a court may need to appoint a Conservator to care for your property. The cost to establish and maintain the conservatorship is charged to you. And that can be very expensive (see Page 237).

☆ TAX SAVINGS

Many people think that the Estate Tax will be phased out so that by 2010, no Estate Taxes will be due regardless of the size of an Estate. That's true for 2010, but the current law covers only the period from 2001 to 2010. The Estate Tax is scheduled to be reinstated on January 1, 2011 and estates worth more than $1,000,000 will once again be subject to a sizeable Estate Tax.

A couple with an Estate in excess of a million dollars can reduce the risk of an Estate Tax by setting up his and her Trusts, so that each person can take advantage of his own exclusion amount. For example, if a couple own 2 million dollars, they can separate their funds into two Trusts each valued at one million dollars. Each Trust can be set up so that a surviving spouse can use the income from the deceased partner's Trust for living expenses. In this way, their standard of living need not be reduced by separating their funds into two Trusts. Once both partners are deceased, the beneficiaries of their respective Trusts will inherit the funds, hopefully with no Estate Tax due.

If the couple do not set up his/her Trusts and continue to hold their property jointly, then the last to die will own the two million dollars with only one tax exclusion available.

☆ PRIVACY

Your Trust is a private document. No one but your Trustee and your beneficiaries need ever read it. If you have a Will and own real property in your name only, or as a tenant in common, then that Will is recorded in the county in Virginia where the property is located (VA 64.1-94). Once recorded, the Will becomes a public document. Anyone can examine the county records, read your Will and see who you did (or did not) provide for in your Will. And records in the Probate Court (inventories, creditor's claims, etc.) are open to public scrutiny. It is not much of a stretch to predict that in the future, Court records will be available on the Internet!

☆ LEASE A SAFE DEPOSIT BOX AS TRUSTEE

Another way to protect your privacy is to lease a safe deposit box in your name as Trustee. This restricts access to the box to you and your Successor Trustee, in the event of your death. If you hold the safe deposit box in your name only and it is necessary for your spouse or next of kin to ask the bank to examine the contents, then a bank officer or employee must be present to examine the contents of the box. By leasing a safe deposit box as Trustee, only you and your Successor Trustee need ever know of the contents of the box.

THE PROBLEMS

With all these perks, you may be ready to call your attorney to make an appointment to set up a Trust, but before doing so there are a few things you need to consider:

☒ COMPLEXITY

A Trust is a fairly complex document, often 20 pages long. It needs to be that long because you are establishing a vehicle for taking care of your property during your lifetime, as well as after your death. Your Trust may be written in "legalese," so it may take you considerable time and effort to understand it. It is important to have your Trust document prepared by an attorney who has the patience to work with you until you fully understand each paragraph of the document and are satisfied that this is what you want.

☒ PROBATE MIGHT STILL BE NECESSARY

The Trust only works for those items that you place in the Trust. If you have property that is held jointly with another, when you die, that property will go to the joint owner and not to the Trust. If you purchase a security in your name only, and forget to put it in your Trust, a Probate procedure may be necessary to determine who should inherit that security. The attorney who prepares the Trust usually creates a safety net for such a situation by having you sign a "Pour Over Will" at the same time you sign your Trust. The purpose of the Will is to "pour" any asset titled in your name only, into the Trust; specifically, the Will directs your Personal Representative to put any asset held in your name only into your Trust. This ensures that all of your property will go to the beneficiaries named in your Trust. But the downside is that a Probate procedure may be necessary to get the asset into the Trust. This defeats a major goal of the Trust, namely to avoid Probate.

⊠ NO CREDITOR PROTECTION FOR GRANTOR

A spendthrift Trust can be set up for a beneficiary (not the Grantor) so that Trust funds are not accessible to the beneficiary's creditors. Creditor protection does not extend to the Grantor of a Revocable Living Trust. Property held in a Revocable Living Trust is freely accessible to the Grantor, it is likewise accessible to his creditors both before and after the Grantor's death. If the Grantor dies owing money, his creditors can have a Personal Representative appointed to locate funds to pay those debts. The Personal Representative can require that the Grantor's Trust property be used to pay for those debts (VA 55-19).

⊠ ☆ THE TRUST IS LEGALLY ENFORCEABLE

Any beneficiary of the Trust can petition a Circuit Court to settle a dispute arising out of the administration of the Trust. The Trustee also has the right to petition the Court for authority to do certain things not authorized in the Trust document. For example, the Trustee can ask the Court to issue an order giving the Trustee authority to terminate the Trust and distribute the Trust property to the beneficiaries (VA 26-1, 55-19.4).

We gave this section a cross and a star, because the right to have a Trust enforced or administered by a court is a double edged sword. It is great to have a court protect the rights of your beneficiaries, but the cost of a court battle could be greater than using Probate to transfer your Estate. Worse yet, your beneficiaries are at a disadvantage because the Trustee can charge the legal expenses to your Trust, while the beneficiaries must pay for their legal battles out of their own pocket. Even if the beneficiaries win the argument, the Trustee's legal fees are paid from the Trust, so there is just that much less for the beneficiaries to inherit.

⊠ TAXES MAY STILL BE A PROBLEM

While the Grantor is operating the Trust as Trustee, all of the property held in a Revocable Living Trust is taxed as if the Grantor were holding that property in his/her own name. If the value of the Trust property exceeds the Estate and Gift Tax exclusion amount (see page 38 for the value), taxes will be due and owing once the Grantor dies. For those in that fortunate tax bracket, an experienced financial planner or tax attorney can suggest other, more advanced, Estate Planning strategies to reduce taxes.

⊠ COST

Because of the thoroughness of the document and the fact that it is custom designed for you, a Trust will cost much more to draft than a simple Will. In addition to the initial cost of the Trust, it can be expensive to maintain the Trust should you become disabled or die. Your Successor Trustee has the right to charge for his duties as Trustee, as well as to charge for any specialized services performed. If you choose an attorney to be Successor Trustee, the attorney has the right to charge to manage the Trust, and also charge for any legal work he performs. A financial institution can charge to serve as Successor Trustee, and also charge to manage the Trust portfolio.

You could appoint a family member who may serve as Successor Trustee for little or no compensation. But regardless of whether you choose a professional or a family member to be Successor Trustee, you need to come to a written agreement as to what will be charged to manage the Trust. The fee agreement can be included in the Trust document or you can have a separate agreement. If you do not make written provision for fees, then under Virginia law, the Trustee (and his attorney) are entitled to be compensated in the same manner as any fiduciary, such as a Personal Representative or a Conservator (VA 26-30).

MAYBE PROBATE ISN'T ALL THAT BAD

Although all of the methods discussed in this Chapter can be used to transfer property without the need for Probate, it may be each method has a downside that is objectionable to you. Maybe you don't have enough money to warrant the cost of setting up the Trust at this time. Holding property jointly with another may raise issues of security and independence. Holding property so that it goes directly to a few beneficiaries in a POD, TOD, or ITF account, may not be as flexible as you wish. This is especially the case if you wish to give gifts to several charities or to minor children instead of just one or two beneficiaries. For example, if you hold all your property so that it goes to your son without the need for Probate, and you ask him to use some of the money for your grandchild's education, it may be that your grandchild gets none of the money because your son is sued or falls upon hard times. If you keep your property in your name only and leave a Will giving a certain amount of money for your grandchild, then the child will know exactly how much money you left and the purpose of that gift.

After taking into account all the pros and cons of avoiding Probate, you may well opt for a Will and a Probate procedure. If you make such a decision, it is important to keep in mind that Estate Planning is not an "all or nothing" choice. You can arrange your Estate so that certain items pass automatically to your intended beneficiary, and other items can be left in your name only, to be distributed as part of a Probate procedure. By arranging your finances in this manner, you can reduce the value of your Probate Estate, and that in turn should reduce the cost of Probate.

YOUR WILL — YOUR WAY

Many people decide that the Will is the best route to go but do not act upon it, thinking it unnecessary to prepare a Will until they are very old and about to die. But according to reports published by the National Center for Health Statistics (a division of the U.S. Department of Health and Human Services) 2 of every 10 people who die in any given year are under the age of 60. Twenty percent may seem like a small number until it hits close to home as it did with a young couple. The couple was having difficulty conceiving a child. They went from doctor to doctor until they met someone just beginning his practice. With his knowledge of the latest advances in medicine, he was able to help them. The birth of their child was a moment of joy and gratitude. They asked a nurse to take a picture of them all together — the proud parents, the newborn child and the doctor who made it all possible. Happiness radiated from the picture, but within 6 months, one of them would be dead.

You might think it was the child. An infant's life is so fragile. SIDS and all manner of childhood diseases can threaten a little one. But no, he grew up a healthy young man.

If you looked at the picture, you might guess the husband. Overweight and stressed out; his ruddy complexion suggested high blood pressure. He looked like a typical heart- attack-prone type A personality.
No, he was fine and went on to enjoy raising his son.

Probably the wife. She had such a difficult time with the pregnancy and the delivery was especially hard. Perhaps it was all too much for her.
No, she recovered and later had two more children.

It was the doctor who was killed in a three car collision.

Though we all agree, that one never knows, still people put off making a Will figuring that if they die before getting around to it, Virginia law will take over and their property will be distributed in the manner that they would have wanted anyway. The problem with that logic is the complexity of the Virginia's Laws of Descent and Distribution. It isn't too difficult to figure out who will inherit your property, if you are survived by a spouse, child, parent or sibling. But if none of these survive you, the ultimate beneficiary of your property may not be the person you would have chosen, had you taken the time to do so.

Others think that it is not necessary to have a Will because they have arranged their finances so that all of their property will be inherited without the need for Probate. But money could come into your Estate after your death. This could happen in any number of ways from winning the lottery and dying (of happiness, no doubt) to receiving insurance funds after your death. For example, if you die in a house fire or flood the insurance company may need to pay for damage done to your property. In such case, a Personal Representative may need to be appointed and the monies distributed according to Virginia law.

If you die without a Will, the Personal Representative may not be the person you would have chosen. The monies may be distributed differently than you would have wished.

And there are other important reasons to make a Will:

ARRANGE FOR PERSONAL REPRESENTATIVE FEES

An important reason to make a Will is so that you can choose your Personal Representative and come to an understanding about how much compensation he is to receive. You can state that value in your Will.

 THE PERSONAL REPRESENTATIVE CAN SEEK MORE MONEY

Your Personal Representative may find the job to be more work than he intended and decide to ask the Commissioner of Accounts to allow a greater value. The Commissioner may think that the amount stated in the Will was the amount you wanted to spend, but not necessarily the amount agreed to by your Representative. To avoid the problem, you can have your attorney draft a binding agreement with your Personal Representative and attach it to your Will. By signing the Agreement, your Personal Representative is promising to accept the fee as provided in the Will.

Having a separate fee agreement will not stop your Personal Representative from asking for more money, but with such an agreement, the Commissioner will not agree to the increase except under extraordinary circumstances.

CHOOSE A GUARDIAN FOR YOUR MINOR CHILD

Either parent has the right to name someone in their Will to be Guardian of their child in the event that the parent dies before the child is grown, and the other parent is unable to care for the child. See the next chapter for more information about how to provide for the care of your minor child.

▤   MAKE GIFTS OF YOUR PERSONAL PROPERTY

Another benefit to making a Will is that you can make provision for who will get your personal property, including your car. If you make a gift of your car in your Will, then it will be relatively simple for your car to be transferred to the beneficiary. If you do not make a specific gift of your car, then it becomes part of your Probate Estate. Your Personal Representative will decide what to do with the car. He can sell it and include the proceeds of the sale in the Estate funds to be distributed to your residuary beneficiaries; or he can give the car to one of the beneficiary of your Estate as part of that beneficiary's share of the Estate.

SMALL GIFTS MATTER

Many who have lost someone close to them report that the distribution of the personal property caused the greatest conflict. If there is no need for a Probate procedure and the decedent died without a Will, then the next of kin need to decide, among themselves, how personal property is to be distributed. Without guidance from the decedent and no Personal Representative with authority to make decisions, there could be much disagreement and hard feelings, as was the case in the example given on page 127.

If you make a Will, you can include the list in your Will and your Personal Representative will distribute your personal property according to your directions. Even if you do not have a Will you can give away your personal property just by making out a list of your possessions, indicating who is receive each item, and then signing the statement (VA 64.1-45.1). It is a good idea to get input from the family when composing your list. You might ask each member of your family to give you a list entitled "THINGS I WOULD LIKE TO HAVE," and then consider all of the lists when you make your decision.

MAKE ADJUSTMENT FOR PRIOR GIFTS

You can make adjustments for gifts or loans given during your lifetime. For example, if you have loaned money to a family member and do not expect to be repaid, then you can deduct the loan from that person's inheritance. Of course, it may be that you are not concerned with inequities. That was the case of an aged woman with three children, Paul, Rita and Frank her youngest. Frank always seemed to need some assist from his mother. She often "lent" him money that he never repaid.

Her other children were responsible and independent. Paul was married and had children of his own. He decided to purchase a house but was having trouble accumulating the down payment. His mother agreed to lend him the money. Paul and his wife offered to give his mother a mortgage on the property. The mother said a simple promissory note from Paul was sufficient, and she would have her attorney draft the note.

The attorney drafted the note but was concerned about the inequity: "You never made a Will. Were you to die, each of your children will inherit an equal amount of money. If Paul still owes money on this promissory note, he will either need to pay the balance to your Estate, or have it subtracted from the amount he inherits. All of the money you gave to Frank will not count towards his inheritance unless you make some adjustment in a Will or unless Frank gives you a promissory note.

"It's O.K." replied the woman "I love all my children equally . . . some a little more equal than others."

STORING YOUR WILL

Once you sign your Will, you may wonder where to store it. Your attorney may offer to store it in his vault. By doing so, he ensures that your heirs will need to contact him as soon as you die. This does not mean that they are required to employ him should a Probate procedure be necessary. It only means that he will have an opportunity for future employment. In exchange, he gives you a good value. Your Will is kept safely in his vault, and at sole cost to him. Should anything happen to that Will, then it is his responsibility to make good the loss. Before allowing your attorney to store the Will, you should get a receipt and something in writing that says:

⇨ The attorney accepts full responsibility for the storage of the Will. Should it be lost or damaged, he will replace the document at no cost to you; and if you are deceased, he will, at no cost to your heirs, present sufficient evidence to the Court to accept a valid copy of the Will into Probate.

⇨ There will be no charge to you, or your heirs, for the storage and retrieval of the document.

With all of this cost and liability, many attorneys will agree only to store a copy of your Will. In such case, consider storing your Will with the Clerk of the Circuit Court in the county of your residence. You are free to retrieve the Will from the Clerk in the event that you move or decide to change your Will.

Regardless of where you choose to store your Will, let your Personal Representative know that you have a Will and how to retrieve it in the event of your death.

THE SAFE DEPOSIT BOX

Many people store their Will or Trust, in a safe deposit box rented from a bank or other financial institution. As Many people store their Will or Trust, and other important documents, in a safe deposit box that they lease from a bank or other financial institution. In Virginia, if you hold a safe deposit box in your name only, access to the box is restricted once you die. Your next of kin can ask the Lessor (usually a bank) of the box to let them inspect the box to see if a Will is in the box. Under Virginia law, the Lessor may allow a spouse or next of kin to look at the contents of the safe deposit box under the supervision of an officer or employee of the company.

If the Will is there, the family member or Lessor can arrange to have it delivered to the Clerk of the Circuit Court. Other than the Will, nothing else can be removed from the safe deposit box without authorization from the Clerk of the Circuit Court (VA 6.1-332.1). A Personal Representative will need to be appointed in order to get possession of the contents of the box. If you have arranged your finances to avoid Probate, then it is self defeating to have entry to a safe deposit box trigger a Probate procedure. To avoid the problem you can:

LEASE THE BOX AS TRUSTEE
As explained, one of the benefits of a Revocable Living Trust is that you can lease the safe deposit box in your name as Trustee. When you lease the safe deposit box you can direct the Lessor (usually a bank) that they are to allow your Successor Trustee free access to the safe deposit box in the event of your incapacity or death.

LEASE THE BOX JOINTLY WITH ANOTHER

If you are married and hold the box jointly with your spouse, then your spouse has free access to the box in the event of your death. If you are single, and do not have a Living Trust, then consider leasing the box jointly with a trusted family member. Of course, if privacy and security are important to you, then that may offset any issue of convenience for your heirs.

APPOINT AN AGENT

You can sign a Power of Attorney giving someone (your Agent) authority to have access to your safe deposit box. The bank usually has forms that you can use give someone that authority, or you can have your attorney draft a Power of Attorney giving someone authority to conduct your business (see Page 239 for a discussion of the Power of Attorney). Under Virginia law, the person your Agent will be able to enter the box up until the time the bank is notified of your death.

CHOOSING THE RIGHT ESTATE PLAN

Joint Ownership?
An "in Trust for" account?
A POD Account?
A TOD Security?
A Trust?
A Will?
An Insurance Policy???

This chapter offers so many options that the reader may be more confused than when he was blissfully unenlightened.

As with most things in life, you may find there are no ultimate solutions, just alternatives. The right choice for you is the one that best accomplishes your goal. This being the case, you first need to determine what you want to accomplish with the money that you leave. Think about what will happen to your property if you were to die suddenly, without making any plan different from the one you now have.

> Who will be responsible to pay your bills?
> Who will get your property?
> Will Probate be necessary?

If the answers to these questions are not what you wish, then you need to work to retitle your property to accomplish your goals.

For those with significant assets, — especially those with estates large enough to pay estate taxes, a trip to an experienced Estate Planning attorney may be well worth the consultation fee.

Continuing To Care 9

There are any number of reasons that people give for wanting to continue on with their life. For the lucky ones, their main reason for living is that they are having a great time and don't want it to end. For many, it is more a sense of responsibility. During child rearing years the concern of the parent is what will happen to the child should the parent suddenly die. Once a child is grown, the roles often reverse, and it is the child worrying about what will happen to his parent if the child were not present to see to the care of the aging parent. Even pet lovers worry about what will happen to their pet should the owner no longer be around.

There is little that can be done to prepare those who depend on you for the loss of your companionship and emotional support; but there are many things you can do to provide financial support for those who rely on you. Even people of modest means can make financial provision so their loved ones will have an easy transition from being dependent to becoming self sufficient.

This chapter explains the many simple, and relatively inexpensive, things you can do to provide care for your loved ones should you not be present to do so yourself.

PROVIDING FOR THE MINOR CHILD

It doesn't happen very often, but both parents could die or become incapacitated before their child reaches adulthood. Most parents don't want to think about, much-less prepare for such a happening. But in this age of postponed parenthood, many parents having children in their thirties and forties and are raising them into their fifties and sixties. The probability of a life threatening illness increases with age, so parents need to understand the importance of planning ahead. Regardless of the parent's age, planning for the care of a minor child should be part of every parent's Estate Plan, not only because it is the responsible thing to do, but also because it is easy and can be done at little cost.

CARING FOR THE PERSON OF THE CHILD

A child must be cared for in two ways, the *person* of the child and the *Estate* (the property) of the child. To care for the person of the child, someone must be in charge of the child's everyday living, not only food and shelter but to provide social, ethical and religious training. Someone must have legal authority to make medical decisions and see to the child's education. If both parents are unable to care for the person of a minor, the Probate court will appoint someone to serve as the child's *Guardian* until the child's 18th birthday.

The Court may have the Guardian care for the child's property, but if the child's assets are significant the Court may decide to appoint a *Conservator* to take charge of the child's property left to the child. The Conservator will be responsible to see that sufficient monies are used for the care of the child and that anything left over is preserved until the child becomes an adult (VA 37.1-134.8).

APPOINTING A GUARDIAN FOR YOUR CHILD

If one parent dies, then it is the right, and duty, of the surviving parent to care for the child (VA 31-1). But it could happen that both parents become incapacitated or die before the child is grown. In Virginia, parents have the right to appoint someone to care for their child in the event that neither of them is able to do so.

As a parent, you have the right to name someone in your Will to serve as your child's Guardian. You can appoint someone to serve as the Guardian of the child's person, and another to serve as the Guardian of the child's property, or you can name someone to serve in both capacities (person and property). The surviving parent has the right to care for the person of your child, so you may want to name the other parent as Guardian of the person, and another as an alternate in the event the other parent is unable to do so.

If you are leaving property for the child in your Will, you can name anyone you wish to serve as the Guardian of that property. The person you name as Guardian of that property has the right to serve in that capacity regardless of whether there is a surviving parent (VA 31-2).

The person you choose as your child's Guardian (person and/or property) can take over in the event anything happens to you, but that person is not the legal Guardian until a Judge of a Circuit Court makes it official. It is important that the person you choose to serve as Guardian be ready and willing to serve, because if that person does not apply within 6 month of your death, then the Court will appoint someone else as Guardian (VA 31-3, 31-14).

LEAVING PROPERTY FOR THE CHILD

As any parent is well aware, it is expensive to raise a child. Someone you think is the best choice to serve as your child's Guardian might not be able to do so unless you leave sufficient monies to pay for the care of the child. If you are a person of limited finances, then consider purchasing a term life insurance policy on your life and/or on the life of the other parent of the child. If you can only afford one policy, then insure the life of the parent who contributes most to the support of the child.

Term insurance policies are relatively inexpensive if you limit the term to just that period of time until your child becomes an adult. Some companies offer a combination of term life and disability insurance. As with any other purchase, it is important to comparison shop to obtain the best price for the coverage.

If you are married, you may want to name your spouse as the beneficiary of the term insurance policy with your child as an alternate beneficiary. Married or single, you can name your child as the primary beneficiary of the policy. If the value of the policy is more than $10,000, the Court may decide to appoint someone to serve as Conservator of the child's Estate (VA 8.01-606).

Conservator procedures can be expensive to set up and maintain. One solution is to appoint a Custodian to care for the insurance proceeds until the child reaches the age of 21. This can be done under the Virginia Uniform Transfers to Minors Act. That Act is explained on the next page.

You can make a gift to a minor in your Will and name someone to be the Custodian of the gift under the Virginia Transfers to Minors Act. Should you die when the child is 21 or older, the property will go directly to the child. If you die before the child is 21, your Personal Representative will deliver the property to the person you named as Custodian. You can even name your Personal Representative to serve as Custodian, and he will hold the property in accordance with the Uniform Transfers to Minors Act (VA 31-41).

This law is designed to protect any gift made to a minor. You can use this method if you want to give a child a gift of a security or a life insurance policy, or even a gift of real property (VA 31-45). Once the gift is made it becomes irrevocable, so this method is not appropriate unless you are sure that you want the child to have the gift once he/she reaches the age of 21. Also, the gift can be made only to one child. If you wish to make a gift to two children, then you will need to make a separate gift to each of them (VA 31-46).

To make a gift under the Virginia Uniform Gifts to Minors Act, you need to name a trusted relative or friend or even a financial institution to be the Custodian of the gift. For example, if you wish to make a gift of an insurance policy on your life, with a financial institution as Custodian, then the owner of the policy can be listed as "ABC BANK as a custodian for _____ (name of minor) under the Virginia Uniform Transfers to Minors Act" (VA 31-48).

The Custodian has the discretion to use the gift to care for the child. The Custodian can pay monies directly to the child, or can use the money for the child's benefit. The Custodian can refuse to use any of the monies for the child and just keep the property or funds invested until it is time to distribute the property. In such case, the child's guardian (or even the child once he/she is 14) can ask a Court to order that the monies be used for the care of the child. The Judge will determine what is in the child's best interest and then rule on the matter (VA 31-50).

Hopefully, the Custodian will give a regular accounting to the child's guardian. If not, any member of the child's family, or the child once he/she reaches 14, can ask the Court to order a full accounting of the custodial property (VA 31-55).

The law requires the Custodian to invest and manage the property in a responsible, prudent manner. The Custodian is entitled to be paid for his effort. If the gift is sizeable, then the Custodian's fee can be sizeable. Before appointing a person or a company as Custodian, it is best to come to a written agreement about how the property will be managed and the charge for doing so (VA 31-51).

The Uniform Transfers to Minors Act is good to use if you want a single gift to be given to a single person once he/she reaches the age of 21. If you want to provide for several children and have more flexibility about when they are to receive the gift, then a Trust may be the better way to go.

 **A TRUST FOR THE CHILD**

If you wish to leave a significant amount of money to someone who is a minor at this time, consider having your attorney prepare a Will for you that contains a Trust for the child. Should you die before the child is grown, monies can be transferred into the child's Trust as part of the Probate procedure. Once the Trust is established, the Commissioner of Accounts will supervise the Trust. Each year he will require that the Trustee file an accounting (VA 26-17.6). The benefit of this arrangement is that there is Court supervision of the Trust. The downside is that it tends to increase the cost of Probate as well as the cost of administering the Trust.

If you have significant funds, the better route might be to set up a Revocable Living Trust. You can fund the Trust while you are alive and bypass Probate altogether. You will handle the Trust funds while you are able. Should you die or become incapacitated whoever you name as Successor Trustee can use the Trust funds to care for the child.

If you are concerned about the management of the Trust funds, you can appoint a financial institution to serve as Successor Trustee. You can instruct the Successor Trustee to use his best discretion to either keep the funds invested until the child reaches a certain age; or to use as much of the funds as necessary to care for the child in the event that the child's parents are unable to do so.

PROVIDING FOR THE STEPCHILD

Perhaps the reason that the story of Cinderella has such universal appeal is that many stepchildren, at one point or another, feel left out. The law seems to reinforce that perception. Should your spouse die, then you, and not your stepchild, have the authority to agree to an autopsy or anatomical gift (see pages 2 and 4). And the law makes no provision for a mandatory inheritance for an adult child. If all of your spouse's property is held jointly with you, then should your spouse die first, your stepchild will be left nothing.

Of course giving you the right to inherit all of your spouse's Estate must be a decision that is agreeable to your spouse. If your spouse wants your step-child to inherit property, then your spouse can arrange his/her finances so that the child will inherit property. Hopefully, your spouse will consult with an Estate Planning attorney who can explain the best way to achieve that goal, else that intent could be thwarted and the child end up with less than your spouse intended, as was the case in the example given on page 120. Also, your spouse has the choice of giving your stepchild the right to make medical decisions and manage your spouse's finances. Your spouse can elect to appoint his/her child as Health Care Agent to make medical decisions in the event that your spouse is unable to do so. And your spouse can give the child Power of Attorney to manage his/her finances in the event that your spouse is unable to do so.

The stepparent often comes across as villain, but it is the parent, and not the stepparent, who decides whether to allow the child's input on medical and financial decisions. And it is the parent, not the stepparent, who decides whether the child shall inherit property belonging to the parent.

THE SECOND MARRIAGE TRUST

A relatively simple solution to the problem of providing for children of a prior marriage is to have a Trust prepared. If you have minor children from a prior marriage, your can have a Trust prepared that will provide funds to care for the children till grown, and at that time, the monies be distributed to your surviving spouse and children in whatever manner you wish. If your children are grown, you may want the income of the Trust to be used to support your surviving spouse; and once the spouse dies, the remainder distributed to your children. A properly drafted Trust can provide for the care of your spouse and child in what ever way you think best.

That was the case with an elderly widower who married a pretty girl one quarter of his age. Their Pre-nuptial Agreement made it clear that all his property would go to his son from his first marriage. Surprisingly, the marriage turned out well. So well that the couple had two daughters. The husband decided to divide his Estate equally between his three children and to provide for the care of his wife until the youngest child was grown.

His attorney suggested a Trust. "You can be Trustee during your lifetime. Once you die, your Successor Trustee can immediately distribute one-third of the Trust to your son who is now 55. No sense to keep him waiting. The rest of your money can remain in your Trust. Income from the Trust can be used to support your wife and children until the youngest is 25. Then, whatever remains in the Trust can be distributed equally to your daughters."

"Good idea" said the elderly gentlemen, with a smile "Just make sure it is revocable during my lifetime. Who knows what adventures I might be up to in the future?"

PROVIDING FOR THE ADULT CHILD

It isn't just stepchildren who can be left out if no provision is made. Even children from a long-standing marriage can be cut off against the wishes of a parent. A parent may assume that all of their children will be treated equally once both parents are gone, but if all their property is held jointly, the last parent to die is the one who gets to decide "who gets what." Too often, the wishes of the deceased parent are ignored, for example:

THE STRAINED RELATIONSHIP: A child may have a close relationship with one parent, and a strained, but tolerable, relationship with the other. Peace in the family is achieved because the parent who is close to the child acts as a buffer. Should the buffer parent die first, then the relationship between the surviving parent and the child may fall apart altogether and the child's inheritance be cut off.

THE PARENT WITH DIMINISHED CAPACITY: The more common scenario, is that the surviving parent becomes increasingly dependent on one child — either for emotional support, or for physical assistance as the parent ages. The other children may live at a distance, or perhaps they are too involved with their own family to assist. The supporting child may end up with most, if not all, of what was intended for all of the children.

These problems can be avoided by having your attorney prepare a Family Trust. The family assets are placed in the Trust with the parents as co-Trustees. The beneficiaries of the Trust cannot be changed unless both parents agree to the change. Once one parent dies, the Trust becomes irrevocable. The Trust income goes to the surviving parent and once that parent dies, whatever remains in the Trust is distributed in the manner as was agreed by both parents.

CARING FOR THE CARETAKER

If you are the caretaker of someone who is incapacitated, then in addition to preparing your own Estate Plan, you need to be concerned about who will care for the incapacitated person should something happen to you. Someone will need to make medical decisions for the incapacitated person and see to it that he/she is properly housed and fed.

APPOINTING A SUCCESSOR CARETAKER

Often a family member will agree to take responsibility for the care of an incapacitated person in the event that the caretaker dies. But perhaps no one wants the job, or the opposite case, too many want to have control. For example, if a parent is incapacitated, one child may want the parent to remain at home with the assistance of a home health care worker. Another child may think the best place for the parent is an assisted living facility with 24 hour care. The caretaker spouse may be concerned that a tug-of-war will erupt once he dies.

There are other problem situations of concern to a caretaker. For example, the parent of an incapacitated child may worry about who will care for the child once the parent is deceased. Or it could be that a parent is seriously ill and is concerned about who will care for their minor child as the parent becomes too ill to care for the child.

In all of these situations, it is appropriate to have a *Standby Guardian* appointed by a Judge of the Circuit Court, as is described on the following page.

 **☎ LAWYER**

APPOINTING THE
STANDBY GUARDIAN

A caretaker parent or spouse can ask the Court to appoint someone to be a Standby Guardian. Once the Standby Guardian is appointed his duties do not begin until the caretaker becomes incapacitated or dies. Up until that point, the caretaker remains in control and does not give up any of his rights because of the appointment (VA 16.1-349).

The caretaker can ask the Court for a Standby Guardian on his own, but it is best to employ an attorney to present evidence to the Court that it is in the best interest of the incapacitated child or spouse, to have a Standby Guardian. In addition to establishing the Standby Guardianship, the attorney will be needed to assist in having the Standby Guardian appointed as permanent Guardian, should the need arise. If the caretaker is without funds, then there are any number of Legal Services who will assist pro bono (see page xiii).

The person chosen by the caretaker to be Standby Guardian must be ready and willing to take over should the need arise. The Standby Guardian will need to apply to be appointed as permanent Guardian within 30 days of the death or incapacity of the caretaker. If the Standby Guardian does not do so within that time, the Court will consider appointing someone else for the job (VA 16.1-351).

 **LAWYER**

A SPECIAL NEEDS TRUST FOR THE INCAPACITATED

If a person is incapacitated, both the federal and state government provide assistance with programs such as Social Security disability benefits and custodial nursing home care under the Medicaid program. The family often supplements the government program by providing for the incapacitated person's *special needs*, such as clothing, hobbies, special education, outings to a movie or a sports event — things that give the incapacitated person some quality of life.

To be eligible for government assistance programs the incapacitated must be essentially without funds. Caretakers fear that leaving money for the incapacitated in a Will or Trust will disqualify the incapacitated from further government assistance. Understanding this dilemma, the federal government allows a parent, grandparent or legal guardian to set up a *Medicaid Special Needs Trust* as authorized by 42 U.S.C. 1396(d)(4) with the incapacitated as the beneficiary of the Trust.

The statute allows the Trustee to use Trust funds to provide for the special needs of the incapacitated. If any funds remain in the Special Needs Trust after the incapacitated dies, then those monies must be used to reimburse the state for monies spent on behalf of the incapacitated person.

An experienced Elder Law attorney can explain the different options available to the family to continue to provide for the incapacitated person's special needs in the event that the caretaker family member dies.

CARING FOR YOUR PET

A woman died at peace,
leaving her fortune
and care of her cat to her niece.
Alas, the fortune and the cat
Soon disappeared after that.

You could leave money to someone with the understanding that the person will take care of your pet, but the moral of the above limerick, is that just leaving money will not guarantee care for your pet.

 ## TRUST FOR CARE OF PET

If you are financially able, you can employ an attorney to set up a Trust for the care of your pet, or you can have the attorney include a trust provision for your pet in your Will.

The person you name as Trustee will be charged with the duty to use Trust funds to pay for the care of your pet. You also need to name a remainder beneficiary (a person or perhaps a charitable organization) to receive whatever remains in the Trust after the pet dies. If you intend the Trustee to also serve as custodian of your pet, then you can ask the remainder beneficiary to regularly check to see that your pet is treated humanely, if not benevolently.

If you don't have the resources to set up a Trust to care for your pet, you can still ask a fellow pet lover to care for the animal. If no one among your circle of family and friends is able to do so, then ask your pet's veterinarian to consider starting an "Orphaned Pet Service" to assist in finding new homes for pets who lose their owners. It is good public relations and a potential source of income. If this is agreeable to the veterinarian, you can make arrangements in your Will to pay the veterinarian to care for the pet until a suitable family can be found. This is a more humane approach than the, all too common practice, of putting a pet "to sleep" rather than have the pet suffer the loss of its master. And in at least one case, that reasoning backfired.

Eleanor always had a pet in the house. After her husband died, her two poodles were her constant companions. When Eleanor became ill with cancer, she worried about what would happen to her "buddies" if she died. She finally decided it best to have her family put them to sleep when she died.

Eleanor endured surgery, chemotherapy, radiation therapy, and even some holistic remedies, but she continued to go downhill. Eleanor's family came in to visit her at the hospital to say their last good-byes. She was so ill, she didn't even recognize them. No one thought she could last the day. Because the family was from out of state, and time short, they decided to put the pets to sleep so they need only take care of the funeral arrangements when she died.

To everyone's surprise, Eleanor rallied. She lived two more long, lonely years.

She often said she wished they had put her to sleep instead of her buddies.

ARRANGING TO PAY BILLS

When people think about their Estate Plan they are more concerned about giving their possessions away than thinking about paying bills. If you are the breadwinner of the family, then you need to think about how your family will manage without you. Eventually, all who are dependent on you will need to fend for themselves, but there are things you can do to help them through the transition period until they become self sufficient. First and foremost is to consider how monies you owe will be paid. If you don't give this some serious thought, then your Estate could be quickly depleted.

If you have significant credit card debt, you need to consider how that debt will be paid once you die. Many credit card companies offer insurance policies with the premium included as part of the monthly payment. If you have such insurance, then should you die, any outstanding balance is paid. It benefits the credit card company to offer life insurance as part of the credit package because they are assured of prompt payment should the borrower die before the debt is paid. However if you have few assets and no one but yourself liable to pay the debt, there is no incentive to pay for insurance that can only benefit the lender.

It is a different matter if you hold a credit card jointly with another person. Both of you are equally liable to pay the debt. Should one of you die, the other is responsible to pay the bill regardless of who ran up the bill. If paying that bill could be a struggle for the surviving debtor, then consider purchasing credit card insurance. If this is not an option because of the cost of the insurance, then the better route might be for each of you to have your own credit card.

Still another reason not to hold a joint credit card is that each of you can establish your own line of credit. This is especially important if you are married and one of you is retired or has been out of the job market for any period of time. Should the breadwinner die, it may be difficult for the surviving partner to establish credit if he/she has no recent work record. It is easier for the unemployed spouse to establish a line of credit when he/she is married to someone who is working.

OTHER TYPES OF LOAN INSURANCE

Most mortgage companies offer mortgage insurance to their borrowers. Mortgage rates are currently low, so an additional charge for mortgage insurance on the life of the primary wage earner may be worth the effort. This is particularly the case with families raising children. With such insurance, the family can inherit the homestead free of debt. The monthly insurance charge may be a small price to pay to ensure that the children can continue to live in their own home until they are grown.

Car loan insurance is still another thing to consider. If a married couple purchase (or lease) a car, and one of them dies, it may be a struggle for the other to pay off the loan. This was the case with Eva and Howard. Both had to work to support their three children. They owned two well used cars. It seemed that one car or the other was always in the shop. When they saw a "NO INTEREST" advertisement for a new car, they decided the offer was too good to pass up. The monthly payments were high, but it was their only luxury. With both their salaries, they were able to make the payments. When Howard had his first heart attack, he was out of work for several weeks so they struggled to keep the payments current.

Howard worked in construction, and was anxious to return to work. The doctors advised that such work might be too strenuous for his weakened heart. Construction work was all Howard knew, and the pay was decent, so he ignored the warning and went back to his job.

The second heart attack was fatal, leaving Eva as the sole means of support for her family. With Howard gone there was no need for two cars. Eva could not afford the payments on the new car so she decided to sell it. Unfortunately, what she could get for the car was significantly less than the balance owed. Once she fell behind in payments she decided to surrender the car rather than have them repossess it. She was sure they would understand, considering she was a widow with three small children.

They didn't.

The company took the car and then sued for the balance of monies owed. The judge was sympathetic, but under the law there is no "life is tough" defense. He ruled that Eva had to pay the monies owed; and, as per the terms of loan agreement, she even had to pay the fees for the company's attorney and all court costs. What an emotional and financial nightmare!

The pity was, it all could have been avoided, had they given it some thought. Howard was the primary driver of the new car and the primary wage earner. All he had to do was to put the loan in his name only, and take out loan insurance. Eva would have inherited the car, debt free. She could have kept it or sold it as she saw fit. Even if Howard didn't purchase loan insurance, had he put the loan in his name only, the company could only have sued his Estate. They would not have been able to sue Eva personally.

PURCHASE LIFE INSURANCE

The good part of purchasing loan insurance — be it credit card insurance, mortgage insurance or car insurance, is that you can usually purchase the insurance without taking a medical examination. The down side is that such insurance may be more expensive than a life insurance policy. If you are in fairly good health, consider taking out a life insurance policy to cover all of your outstanding loans. The cost of the single life insurance policy may be significantly less than purchasing separate loan insurance policies.

The Estate Planning strategy of purchasing life insurance to pay off all of your loans works best if you are married and your spouse is jointly liable for your debts. If you name your spouse as beneficiary of the life insurance policy, then he/she can use the life insurance funds to pay off all monies owed. If you name your spouse or child and that person has no legal obligation to pay your debts, then none of your creditors can force your beneficiary to use any part of those funds to pay your debts, unless you purchased the insurance policy to defraud your creditors. If your creditor can prove that such was your intent, then the creditor can require that whatever you paid to purchase the policy, plus interest, be subtracted from the insurance proceeds and be used to pay your debt (VA 38.2-3122).

If you want the insurance funds used to pay your debts, then leaving the money to someone who has no duty to pay the debt is not the way to go. But, if you want to be sure that someone receives money for their care after you are gone, then purchasing life insurance should accomplish your goal.

With or without debt, you may be wondering about life insurance — should you have it? How much is enough? The answer to these questions depends on the "sleep at night" factor, namely how much insurance do you need to make you not worry about insurance coverage when you go to sleep at night? It is often more an emotional than a financial issue.

Some people have an "every man for himself" attitude and are content to have no life insurance at all. When they die, whatever they have, they have. And that is what their heirs will inherit. Others worry about how their loved ones will manage if they are not around to support them, and decide to purchase enough insurance to maintain their dependents in their accustomed life style.

The same person may have different thoughts about insurance coverage as the circumstances of their life changes — from no coverage in their bachelor days to more-than-enough coverage in their child rearing days to just-enough-to-bury-me in their senior years.

Insurance companies recognize that people's needs change over the years. Many companies offer flexible insurance coverage. As with any consumer item, it is a good idea to shop around.

| Special Situation | PROVIDING FOR THE FAMILY BUSINESS |

If you are the sole proprietor of a business, then you need to give considerable thought to what will happen to that business in the event of your incapacity or death. Can the business continue to operate without you? Is it your intent that whoever inherits your business take over its daily operations or do you think it best to have the business sold and have the proceeds of the sale given to your beneficiaries? If you do not make provision for the orderly transfer of your business, then your Personal Representative or a Probate Court may need to make that decision for you.

In addition to the running of the business you need to consider how company debts will be paid. If your business is highly leveraged (business talk for "owes lots of money"), you also need to consider how those loans will be paid should you become disabled or die.

Taxes are still another concern. Your business may be worth millions on paper, and your Estate taxes will be based on that value. You heirs may be forced to sell the company just to pay the taxes, but without your leadership they may get only a fraction of the value of the company. A solution to the problem is to purchase a key man or life insurance policy to pay taxes and get the company through the transition period.

An attorney or a financial planner who is experienced in business matters can offer other suggestions as to the best method of ensuring that the business continues its operation, or terminates in an orderly fashion — whichever is applicable in your case.

ESTATE PLANNING FOR THE BANKRUPT

You may think the above title to be an oxymoron (a contradiction in terms). If a person is bankrupt, why plan for an Estate he doesn't have? But facts are, that people who file for bankruptcy are often quite wealthy and that is their downfall. Because they have substantial income or property, banks and people are willing to lend them money. If more money is borrowed than can be repaid, the unhappy result is bankruptcy. In the event that you are concerned about meeting your responsibilities as parent or spouse, yet you enjoy a life style of financial brinkmanship, then consider investing in items that are "creditor proof."

That's exactly what Alan decided to do. Alan was astute, well aware of his strengths and weaknesses. He enjoyed his work and knew he had the capacity to earn large sums of money. But he also knew he was a gambler. Not the Las Vegas type, but a gambler in business ventures. "No risk, no gain" was one his favorite sayings.

If you charted Alan's net worth over the years it would look like the peaks and valleys of the NASDAQ. Lots of high highs and low lows. Unfortunately, he married a woman who did not share his adventurous spirit. His wife became increasingly intolerant of their financial instability. She came to realize that this was his life style and things would never change. "All gamblers die broke," she said as she walked out the door with their 5 year old daughter in tow.

That, and the fact that he had to declare bankruptcy, brought Alan up short; and he began to be concerned about his future and that of his family.

Alan talked things over with his bankruptcy attorney "I am a good businessman, but not a clairvoyant. There was no way to predict the turn of events that led to this situation. But I know I will bounce back, and it will just be a matter of time before I am earning a good living. I also know that I am an entrepreneur and not a 9 to 5 type guy so this could happen again. What concerns me is how to provide some security for my child in the event that something happens to me before she is grown."

His attorney's response was a surprise:
"Move to another state."

"You're kidding."

"Not really. There are few items in Virginia that are creditor proof. You could prepay your daughters tuition and no creditor can reach that. You might consider saving for your retirement. A pension plan is a good Estate Planning tool. Although here in Virginia, the amount that is creditor proof depends on your life expectancy (VA 34-34). At your age, the most you can protect is $100,000. In other states, there is an unlimited amount of protection."

Alan didn't think that would work. "I am my own boss, and I don't have the self discipline to put money aside each month for my retirement."

The attorney suggested "Up to $5,000 of the value of your homestead is exempt from your creditors during your lifetime (VA 34-4). Should you die, your wife and child are entitled to up to $10,000 as a Homestead Allowance free of your creditors (VA 64.1-151.3). Other states have no limit on homestead creditor protection. For example, if you buy a home in Florida and make it your principal residence, then regardless of what you pay for the house, your daughter can inherit it free from the claims of your creditors (with certain exceptions such as mechanic's liens and mortgages). The legislature is considering putting a cap on the amount that can be shielded from creditors in this way, but as of this date there's no limit."

The attorney continued "You could purchase a life insurance policy and your daughter will inherit the proceeds free of your debts. I don't recommend you buy the policy right now. If you purchase the policy now that you are insolvent (i.e., you owe more than you own), then should you die, your creditors can demand that the monies paid for the policy (plus interest) be given to them and not to your daughter. But only the premium (what you paid for the policy) is at risk; so if the premium is just a small part of the proceeds, then maybe this is not of concern to you.

Another problem with purchasing a life insurance policy, is that if you get into serious financial difficulties during your lifetime, your creditors could force you to cash in the policy to pay your debt. There is a way around both these problems by setting up an Irrevocable Insurance Trust. The Trustee purchases the policy. You are the insured person, but the Trust is the owner of the policy. When you are ready to do some serious Estate Planning, we can get together and discuss some sophisticated Estate Planning strategies."

ANNUITIES TO SPREAD THE INHERITANCE

Some people have difficulty accumulating money to leave to their heirs. Some heirs have difficulty hanging on to their inheritance. It is not uncommon for an heir to go through his inheritance within two years. For many, the reason the money is gone so soon, is that there just wasn't much money to inherit in the first place. But for others, it's a spending frenzy.

People's spending habits remain much the same throughout their lifetime. Some people are squirrels, always saving for the winter. For others, it's:

Earn-A-Penny   Spend-A-Penny

Most of us fall somewhere in between. We are not extravagant in our spending habits, yet it is a struggle to save. A person such as Alan, in the example just given, might wonder why he should struggle to purchase an insurance policy if he knows the intended beneficiary will spend it all within a few months?

If you want to leave an insurance policy benefit to someone you love, but the intended beneficiary is immature, or a born spendthrift, then a simple solution to the problem may be to purchase an annuity rather than life insurance. An annuity is a type of insurance policy that can be set up so that your beneficiary (the *annuitant*) receives money on a monthly, or yearly basis, rather than a single lump sum payment when you die. You can even set up the annuity so that it is protected from the creditors of the beneficiary. Virginia law allows up to one million dollars to be so protected (VA 55-19).

An annuity can also be set up to benefit your favorite charity, and to reduce, if not eliminate the Capital Gains Tax. For example, suppose you own several acres of land in West Virginia that you purchased many years ago. You may have been putting off selling the property because of the Capital Gains Tax. But it has been a liability to you. It produces no income and because the property continues to appreciate, each year, you are paying more and more in property taxes. If you are living on a pension income, it makes no sense to continue to pay money in property taxes, when that money could be used to give you additional income. A solution to the problem is to donate the property to your favorite charity with an agreement that they will sell the property and use the money to purchase an annuity that will give you an income for your life. The agreement is called the *Charitable Remainder Annuity Trust*.

A Charitable Remainder Annuity Trust is a Trust that is established according to the Internal Revenue Code (IRC 664). Charities do not pay taxes, so property donated to the Trust can be sold by the Trustee free of the Capital Gains Tax. The money from the sale is invested so that it provides an income (an annuity) to you either for a fixed period of time, say 20 years, or for your lifetime as computed by actuarial tables (i.e., your estimated life expectancy). It can even be set up so that the annuity continues to be paid to your spouse after your death.

How much income you receive, and how much goes to the charity, depends on several factors including the value of the donated property and the length of time the annuity is paid. Your financial planner or Estate Planning attorney can suggest the type of Charitable Trust that best meets your goals.

A downside is the cost of setting up the plan. It may cost significant attorney fees to set up the Trust. Some charities may offer to have their attorney prepare the Trust at no cost to you, or perhaps they offer a "standard" Trust document that their attorney prepared. But their Trust was prepared by an attorney for the greatest benefit to his client (that's the charity, not you). It is important that you employ your own attorney to represent you. He knows the extent of your Estate and he understands what you wish to accomplish. Once established, the Trust is irrevocable, so it is important that you understand all of the aspects of the Trust, including what income taxes will need to be paid by the annuitant.

If you decide to set up a Charitable Remainder Annuity Trust, then the benefits to you are many:

☑   TAX SAVINGS

You will no longer need to pay annual property taxes. And the full value of the donated property is used to set up the annuity. Had you sold the property and invested the money yourself, you would have had to pay a Capital Gains Tax and that tax could be substantial, depending on the tax rate in effect at the time of the transfer. By gifting the property the full value of the land can be used to produce investment income. And because the transfer represents a gift to the charity, you even get to take a charitable deduction on your income tax return in the year the property is transferred into the Trust.

☑   NO PROBATE EXPENSE

Because the land is in a different state, it could be both time consuming and expensive to transfer the property to your beneficiaries upon your death. By donating the property to the Trust, you avoid the need for a Probate procedure in another state.

☑   CREDITOR PROTECTION

If you keep the land and are sued, you could lose it to pay your creditors. If your spouse inherited the land, it could be lost to creditors. But once the property is transferred into the Trust, the gift is made. Neither your creditors nor the creditors of any successor annuitant of the Trust can get access to the Trust property. The most the creditor can do is ask for payment from the money received as an income.

☑   SPENDTHRIFT PROVISION

If your spouse is a spendthrift and inherited the land, all of the money could be spent in short order. You can set up this annuity Trust for the benefit of your spouse and be assured that your spouse will have a steady income over a long period of time.

☑   GIVE WHEN NEEDED INSTEAD OF LATER

A Charitable Remainder Annuity Trust can be set up in any number of different ways to accommodate your Estate Plan. For example, if you are not in need of a present income, but expect that you will spend significant sums on your child's education, you can set up a 20 year annuity with your child as the annuitant. This will get the child through college and probably be a great help should the child decide to start a family. Why have the child inherit property in later, high earning years rather than in the early, high expense/low income years?

☑   GOOD DEED

Whatever is left of the donation after payment of the annuity goes to your favorite charity. By making a donation to the charity of your choice, you are sharing your good fortune with others. You can consider this as "giving back" to the community, or just plain doing a good deed.

A Health Care Estate Plan 10

The last two chapters discussed the distribution or management of your Estate once you are deceased. But in this age of an extended life expectancy, a more important topic is how to manage and preserve your Estate in the event of a debilitating illness. As life expectancy increases, so does the percentage of the population who suffer incapacity from debilitating strokes, Alzheimer's disease or Parkinsons' disease. It is estimated that more than 50% of the population who are 85 or older, suffer some degree of dementia. Your best Estate Plan could be sabotaged by lengthy or incapacitating illness.

If you are concerned that you may become disabled in the future, you need to consider who will care for your person and who will take care of your property. In Chapter 7 we discussed how you can appoint Health Care Agent to make your medical decisions in the event that you are too ill to do so yourself. You Health Care Agent will care for your person in the event of your incapacity. But there is still the problem of who will care for your property.

In this chapter we will discuss a Health Care Estate Plan to preserve and protect your finances during your lifetime. We will discuss how you can appoint someone to handle your finances in the event of your incapacity, and how you can arrange to pay for the health care you may require as you age.

A TRUST TO CARE FOR PROPERTY

The optimum way to provide for the care of your property in the event of your incapacity, is to set up a Trust appointing a Successor Trustee to care for your property according to the directions given in your Trust. You can be Trustee of the funds while you have capacity. Should you become incapacitated, then the person you name as Successor Trustee will take over. If you are a person of substance, then you should consider having an attorney design a Trust especially for you.

You may be wondering what we mean by the term "a person of substance." We have avoided defining the term because wealth is a state of mind. If you think back on your life, you can probably recall times of well being, where you felt on top of the world and a fortunate person. Excluding winners of game shows and the lottery, for most of us, the moment we felt most wealthy did not coincide with the high point of our net worth.

Except for the extremes of Bill Gates and a homeless person, whether you are poor or wealthy depends more on your subjective perception than any objective standard. Using this subjective standard, you should have a Trust prepared when you feel rich enough to conclude that the benefits of a Trust justify the cost of preparing and maintaining the Trust. And just to keep things grounded in reality, take an objective view of your finances by determining your *Net Worth* (the cash value of your assets, less the amount of monies you owe).

You can use the form on the next page to calculate that value. If you are married and hold all property jointly, then calculate the Net Worth of all of the assets and divide by 2, for your own Net Worth.

DETERMINING YOUR NET WORTH

ASSETS:

$ _____ Cash (coin collection, bank accounts,
                                     certificates of deposit, etc.)

$ _____ Cash value of insurance policies

$ _____ Securities (stocks, bonds, mutuals, etc.)

$ _____ Pension Plans, IRA's, etc.

$ _____ Cash value of a partnership or other
                                     business interest

$ _____ Tangible personal property (jewelry,
                                     private art or stamp collections,
                                     motor vehicles, etc.)

$ _____ Real property (residences, vacant
                                     lots, condominiums, cooperatives,
                                     time shares, etc.)

$ _____ TOTAL VALUE OF ASSETS

It may be that you and the bank own all of this, so you need to subtract away monies that you owe on any of the above items:

LIABILITIES

$ _____ Private loans
$ _____ Mortgage Balance
$ _____ Credit card debt
$ _____ Car loan or car lease balance
$ _____ TOTAL LIABILITIES

A simple subtraction gives you your *net worth*:
        ASSETS — LIABILITIES = NET WORTH

THE CONVENIENCE ACCOUNT

If you do not have sufficient assets to justify the cost of employing an attorney to draft a Trust, and you are concerned that at some time in the future you may become incapacitated and unable to handle your finances, then there are strategies, other than a Trust, that you can use to solve the problem.

THE CONVENIENCE ACCOUNT

You can set up your checking account so that a trusted family member can write checks on the account. Of course there are all the inherent problems of a joint account that we discussed on page 177. You can avoid many of those problems by limiting the amount of money that can be accessed by the family member. For example, you can arrange your finances so that all of your bills are paid from a single checking account and your family member can access that account, only.

If you set up a joint account, your family member will own whatever is in the account should your die. If this is not as you wish, you can instruct the bank that this is a convenience account and that in the event of your death the family member may no longer access your account. But ultimately the family member must be trustworthy because the bank is under no duty to stop your family member from writing checks on your account until the bank learns of your death.

The joint or convenience account solves the problem of how to pay your bills in the event you are temporarily ill. It does not solve the problem of how to manage your business affairs in the event of an extended illness. For example, suppose you have a stroke and can no longer be cared for at home. Should it be necessary for you to sell your home and move to an assisted living facility, then no one will have the authority to sell the house for you. In such case, the Court will need to appoint someone (a *conservator*) to manage your finances, and probably a guardian to make your medical decisions.

The person appointed as your guardian and/or conservator is entitled to be paid for his services. The amount paid must be approved by the Court. As fiduciaries, they are entitled to compensation just the same as any fiduciary such as a Personal Representative or a Trustee. The duties of a conservator are the same as those of a Personal Representative. He must take possession of your assets, file an inventory with the Court, and each year, account to the Court for monies spent. The Court may decide that a bond is necessary for the protection of your assets. If so, he will order the Conservator to obtain a bond.

As with a Personal Representative, the conservator or guardian needs to employ an attorney to establish the conservatorship and/or guardianship and then see to it that it is properly administered. Attorney's fees must be approved by the Court. The hourly rate is much the same as the Court awards to attorneys to administer a Probate Estate. Court filing fees, the cost of a bond, attorney's fees, guardian and conservator fees, all are paid from your Estate (that's your money!) (VA 37.1-134.16, 37.1-137.2).

Conservator and guardianship procedures are expensive to set up and maintain. Curious that so many people worry about how to avoid Probate, when the larger concern should be how to avoid guardianship or conservatorship proceedings. Consider that it is not all that hard to arrange your finances so that no Probate is necessary. The cost to administer your Estate should be $0. Even with a full Probate procedure, the administration usually ends within a year.

Whatever it costs to Probate your Estate is a one-time expense. Once monies are distributed to the beneficiaries, it is ended. Not so if you become incapacitated. It can cost thousands of dollars to set up the guardianship and/or conservatorship; and more money to care for your and your property each year.

The Conservator must manage your money, and work with his attorney to prepare an annual accounting to the Court. The guardian must see to your health care, and work with his attorney to prepare an annual report to the Court regarding your well-being. The guardian and the Conservator (and their attorneys) are entitled to reasonable compensation for these services. Even if the same person serves as guardian and conservator, and there is only one attorney, the cost to your Estate is sizable. And this expense continues year after year until you are returned to capacity, or die.

As with Probate it is not all that hard to avoid these unnecessary charges to your Estate. One way to avoid guardianship procedures is to appoint a Health Care Agent to make your medical decisions should you be too ill to do so yourself (see page 170). There are several ways to avoid a conservatorship. A Trust is the best vehicle. For those of limited means, a Power of Attorney is the next best Estate Plan.

A POWER OF ATTORNEY FOR FINANCES

A Power of Attorney is a legal document by which someone (the **Principal**) gives another (his **Agent** or **Attorney-In-Fact**) authority to do certain acts on behalf of the Principal. If you wish to have someone to be able to conduct business on your behalf in the event of your incapacity, then you can make the Power of Attorney **durable** by adding the phrase "This Power of Attorney shall not terminate on the disability of the Principal" (VA 11-9.1).

You can give your Attorney-In-Fact general powers to manage your finances, to do much the same with your property as you can do yourself, such as:

⇨ sell any of your real or personal property;

⇨ buy real or personal property for you;

⇨ trade in securities;

⇨ pay your bills and/or taxes;

⇨ operate your business;

⇨ have access to your safe deposit box;

⇨ borrow money on your behalf;

⇨ purchase insurance policies and name beneficiaries;

⇨ sue or defend a law suit on your behalf.

You can even give your Attorney-In-Fact power to make gifts of your property in accordance with your Estate Plan, for example, you can direct him to give certain family members up to $10,000 in gifts each year (VA 11-9.5).

Instead of giving your Attorney-In-Fact broad general powers, you can limit the things he can do with your property to just one or two things that you authorize in your Power of Attorney.

Limited or general, the operative word in any Power of Attorney is POWER. Once your Attorney-In-Fact has authority to act, he essentially steps in your shoes and can do whatever you gave him authority to do. Your primary consideration in choosing an Agent is trustworthiness. You need to choose someone who will follow your instructions and put the Power of Attorney to the use you intended. You need to choose someone, who, when using your Power of Attorney, will always put your interests ahead of his.

Perhaps you are less concerned with trustworthiness than the loss of your independence. You may want to give someone a Power of Attorney, but not until it is needed. This presents a dilemma. If you wait until it is needed, you may be too sick to sign the document. There are two simple solutions.

KEEP THE DOCUMENT IN YOUR POSSESSION

Before anyone (a bank, stockbroker, closing agent, etc.) will accept the Power of Attorney they will want to see the original document so that they are assured that your Attorney-In-Fact has authority to transact business on your behalf. If you keep the original document in your possession and do not give anyone a copy, your Attorney-In-Fact will not be able to act for you.

The only problem with this arrangement is that you need to arrange to make the document accessible to your Agent in the event of your incapacity. If your Agent is a trusted family member, then you can give your Agent the location of the document with instructions to take possession of the Durable Power of Attorney in the event of your incapacity.

A better solution may be to have your attorney draft a "springing" Durable Power of Attorney that is not operational until your family doctor and/or independent physician says that you are incapacitated and unable to manage your financial affairs. Your Attorney-In-Fact can hold the original document, but cannot use it until it "springs to life" when a doctor determines that you are too ill to care for your property (VA 11-9.4).

USING THE POWER OF ATTORNEY FOR MEDICAL DECISIONS
Your attorney can design a Durable Power of Attorney, to meet your special needs. He can even include powers that relate to your health care. But as a practical matter, it may be better to have a separate document drafted to appoint a Health Care Agent. You can have your attorney draft an Advance Medical Directive appointing a Health Care Agent and giving specific instructions about the type of medical treatment you wish if you are too ill to speak for yourself (see Page 170). Your Health Care Agent will give a copy of your Advance Medical Directive to your physician to be placed in your medical file. Your doctors have no need to know of your business dealings.

The Durable Power of Attorney gives your Attorney-In-Fact authority to handle your business matters. To conduct business on your behalf your Attorney-In-Fact will need to give a copy of the document to your business associates (banks, stockbrokers, etc.). Your business associates have no need to know of your medical decisions.

For privacy, and perhaps security reasons, consider having a separate document prepared for your health care (the Advance Medical Directive) and another for your finances (a Durable Power of Attorney), rather than try to get it all into a single all purpose document.

It is relatively simple and inexpensive to head off guardianship or conservatorship proceedings. All you need do is appoint an Attorney-In-Fact under a Durable Power of Attorney to manage your finances, and a Health Care Agent under an Advance Medical Directive to make your medical care decisions. These documents authorize people of your choice to care for you and your property in the event of your incapacity. But, despite your best plans, something unusual could happen causing a Court to decide that you need a guardian or a Conservator. For example, suppose you disappear and cannot be found after a diligent search. It might be necessary to have a Court appoint a Conservator to protect your property in your absence. Or perhaps you develop an addiction or a mental illness causing self-destructive behavior. Your friends or family might decide that you are in need of protection and ask a Court to determine whether you are incapacitated, i.e., unable to care for yourself, and if so, then to appoint a guardian to care for you (VA 37.1-134.8).

Although it may not be possible to avoid all guardianship and conservatorship proceedings, if you have appointed a Health Care Agent under an Advance Medical Directive and an Agent under a Durable Power of Attorney you can have some measure of control in your fate. Your Health Care Agent will continue to make your medical decisions in accordance with the directions given in your Advance Medical Directive. Your Attorney-In-Fact will continue to manage your finances in the manner you directed in your Power of Attorney. Whoever is appointed as guardian cannot override the authority given in these document unless he goes to Court and gets the Judge's permission. The Judge will not revoke or modify your Medical Directive or Power of Attorney unless there is some pressing need to do so (VA 11-9.1, 37.1-137.1).

PROVIDING FOR LONG TERM CARE

The good news is: You are going to live longer.
The bad news is: It's going to cost you.

Scientists are doing a great job of prolonging life, but
unless they find Ponce De Leon's fountain, the general
population will age. Along with age comes infirmities.
Eyes fail. Hearing diminishes. Nervous systems
deteriorate. Digestive systems either speed up or slow
down, all to the discomfort of the unhappy occupant of
the body. It's all part of the "golden" years.

The pharmacology industry is well motivated to produce
drugs that manage the ills associated with aging. Their
research has led to a wealth of pharmaceutic products
that do not cure, but do allow people to live relatively
comfortably into advanced age. The only problem is the
cost of these drugs. Medicare covers the treatment of
life-threatening brushes with heart disease, stroke, cancer
and diabetes; but, as of this writing, Medicare does not
pay for maintenance medication that is often necessary
once the condition is stabilized.

Medicare is also limited in long term health care coverage.
It does not pay for extended nursing care. Medicare pays
for the first 20 days of skilled nursing care. Medicare pays
the excess over $99 for days 21 through 100. That means
you pay $7,920 for the next 80 days. After 100 days, you
are on your own. A nursing home stay of one or two years
can wipe out the life savings of most working people.
Once savings are gone, the government provides care in
the form of Medicaid coverage.

If you are poor, long-term nursing care may not be of concern to you, because all your needs should be covered under Medicaid. If you are very wealthy, you may not worry because you have more than enough money to pay for your care. But the rest of us need to think about ways to provide for long-term health care. For those concerned about the loss of life savings because of illness, there is supplemental and/or long-term health care insurance. There are many different insurance plans available. You can call the National Association of Insurance Commissioners at (816) 842-3600 and they will forward to you, free of charge, the publication:

A SHOPPER'S GUIDE TO LONG TERM CARE INSURANCE

If you have a specific question, you can call the Virginia Department of Aging at (804) 662-9333.

FOR FEDERAL EMPLOYEES/RETIREES

The Long Term Care Security Act (Public Law 106-265) was passed by Congress to take effect in October, 2002. The law is designed to make long-term care insurance available to Federal employees, members of the uniformed services, and civilian and military retirees. The Office of Personnel Management is currently at work establishing the terms of the policy and determining the cost of the insurance policy to federal employees or retirees. You can download a copy of the law from their Web site:

 OFFICE OF PERSONNEL MANAGEMENT
http://www.opm.gov/insure/ltc

The National Association Of Retired Federal Employees ("NARFE") has been actively involved in this new legislation. You can get updates on the law by calling their legislative hotline in Alexandria, Virginia at (703) 838-7780, or by visiting their Web site:

 NARFE WEB SITE
http://www.narfe.org

MEDICAID ESTATE PLANNING

Many people find themselves in the unhappy position of being uninsurable because of a pre-existing condition, or perhaps without sufficient income to pay for long term health insurance coverage. The worst case scenario is a person who has a serious illness and is too rich for Medicaid and too poor to afford nursing care without depleting their life savings.

People in this situation may decide to divest themselves of all property and hope that they will not need extended nursing care for at least three years. Once three years have passed, they hope to be eligible for Medicaid. For most, their motives are altruistic. The money is given to a child to keep safe for the parent, but what the parent is really trying to do is protect the child's inheritance.

The parent may rationalize: "I worked all my life and hoped to leave a few pennies for the kids. Why did I work so hard? To give it all to a nursing home? Why should I use all of my life savings to pay for a few years of nursing care? Doesn't the government pay hundreds of thousands of dollars for people on Medicare to have open heart surgery, or to pay for lengthy and expensive cancer treatments? Why should people who suffer from the effects of a severe stroke, or from Alzheimer's or from Parkinsons not be entitled to receive similar benefits for their disease?"

And so they give all of their money away.

Giving away all assets and then waiting three years is what this author considers to be a "Brute Force" Medicaid Estate Plan. There's no finesse. It is a drastic step to take and fraught with perils. The obvious problems are ones we mentioned before when discussing the transfer of the homestead.

What if the child is sued?

What if the child gets married, or divorced?

What if the child falls on hard times?

But the real problem is the loss of independence. Being impoverished at a time in your life when you are unable to supplement your income, and when your physical health is declining, can lead to much sadness. Imagine going to your child and asking for money. Imagine the child thinking, or worse yet, asking,

"What is the money for?"

Before divesting yourself of your assets, or if you are the child, before you accept those assets, consult with an experienced Elder Law attorney. In many cases, there are other, better, strategies.

 Medicaid Estate Planning is a specialty. The attorney must know all of the federal and state laws relating to the subject. In addition, the attorney needs to know what strategies are liable to be challenged should the person need to apply for Medicaid. Before employing an attorney, determine what percentage of his practice is devoted to Medicaid Estate Planning and how long he has practiced in the field of Elder Law.

Your Estate Plan Record 11

Once you are satisfied with your Estate Plan, then the final thing to consider is whether your heirs will be able to locate your assets once you are deceased.

Most people have their business records in one place, their Will in another place, car titles and deeds in still another place. When someone dies, their beneficiaries may feel as if they are playing a game of "hide and seek" with the decedent. The game might be fun if it were not for the fact that things not found may be forever lost. For example, suppose you die in an accident and no one knows you are insured by your credit card company for accidental death in the amount of $25,000. The only one to profit is the insurance company, which is just that much richer because no one told them that you died as a result of an accident.

And how about a key to a safe deposit box located in another state? Will anyone find it? Even if they find the key, how will they find the box?

It is not difficult to arrange things so that your affairs are always in order. It amounts to being aware of what you own (and owe) and keeping a record of your possessions. A side benefit is that by doing so, you will always know where all your business records are. If you ever spent time trying to collect information to file your taxes or trying to find a lost stock or bond certificate, you will appreciate the value of organizing your records.

ORGANIZING YOUR RECORDS

Heirs need all the help they can get. It is difficult enough dealing with the loss, without the frustration of trying to locate important documents. Your heirs will have no problem locating your assets if you keep all of your records in a single place. It can be a desk drawer or a file cabinet or even a shoe box. It is helpful if you keep a separate file or folder for each type of investment. You might consider setting up the following folders:

📂 THE BANK & SECURITIES FOLDER

Store your original certificates for stocks, bonds, mutual funds, certificates of deposit, in a folder labeled **BANK & SECURITIES FOLDER**. In addition to the original certificate include a copy of the contract you signed with each financial institution. The contract will show where you have funds and who you named as beneficiary or joint owner of the account. If someone owes you money and has signed a Promissory note or mortgage that identifies you as the lender, then you can store these documents in this folder as well.

If you wish to store your original documents in a safe deposit box, then keep a record of the location of the safe deposit box, and the number of the box, in this folder. Make a copy of all of the items stored in the box and place the copies in this folder. If you have an extra key to the box, then put the key in the folder. If you are the only person with access to the box, it may take a probate procedure to remove items from the box once you die. Consider allowing someone you trust to be able to gain entry to the box in the event of your incapacity or death.

📁 THE DEED FOLDER

Many people save every scrap of paper associated with the closing of real property. If you closed recently on real estate and there was a mortgage involved in the purchase, you probably walked away from closing with enough paper to wallpaper your kitchen. If you wish, you can keep all of those papers in a separate file that identifies the property, for example: CLOSING PAPERS FOR ROANOKE CONDO

Set aside the original deed (or a copy if the original is in a safe deposit box) and place it into a separate DEED FOLDER. Include deeds to parcels of real property, cemetery deeds, condominium deeds, cooperative shares to real property, timesharing certificates, etc. Include deeds to out of state property as well as Indiana property in the DEED FOLDER. If you have a mortgage on your property, then put a copy of the mortgage and promissory note in a separate LIABILITY FOLDER.

📁 THE LIABILITY FOLDER

The LIABILITY FOLDER should contain all loan documents of debts that you owe. For example, if you purchased real property and have a mortgage on that property, then put a copy of the mortgage and promissory note in this folder. If you owe money on a car, put the loan documents in the file. If you have a credit card, put a copy of the contract you signed with the credit card company in this file. Many people never take the time to calculate their net worth (what a person owns less what that person owes). By having a record of your assets and outstanding debts, you can calculate your net worth whenever you wish.

📁 THE INSURANCE FOLDER

The **INSURANCE FOLDER** is for each original insurance policy that you own, be it car insurance, homeowner's insurance or a health care insurance policy. If you purchased real property, you probably received a title commitment at closing and the original title insurance policy some weeks later when you received your original deed from recording. If you cannot locate the title insurance policy, then contact the closing agent and have them send you a copy of your title policy.

📁 THE PENSION AND ANNUITY FOLDER

If you have a Pension or Annuity, then put all of the documents relating to the Pension in this folder. Include the telephone number and/or address of the person to contact in the event of your death.

FOR FEDERAL RETIREES If you are a Federal Retiree, you should have received your **PERSONAL IDENTIFICATION NUMBER (PIN)** and the person who will inherit your pension (your *survivor annuitant*) should have received his/her own PIN as well. It is relatively simple to obtain this during your lifetime, but it may be difficult and/or stressful for your survivor annuitant to work through the system once you are gone.

Survivor annuitant benefits are not automatic. Your survivor annuitant must apply for them by submitting a death claim to the Office of Personnel Management. Your survivor needs to know that it is necessary to apply and also how to apply. You can get printed information about how apply for benefits from the Office Of Personnel Management. (see Page 30). Keep the printed information in this file.

🗁 THE PERSONAL PROPERTY FOLDER

MOTOR VEHICLES Put all motor vehicle titles in a Personal Property folder. This includes cars, mobile homes, boats, planes, etc. If you owe money on the vehicle, the lender may have possession of the title certificate. If such is the case, then put a copy of the title certificate and registration in this folder and a copy of the promissory note or chattel mortgage in a separate liability folder. If you have a boat or plane, then identify the location of the motor vehicle. For example, if you are leasing space in an airplane hanger or in a marina, keep a copy of the leasing agreement in this file.

JEWELRY   If you own expensive jewelry, keep a picture of the item together with the sales receipt or written appraisal in this folder.

COLLECTOR'S ITEMS If you own a valuable art or coin collection, or any other item of significant value, include a picture of the item in this file. Also include evidence of ownership of the item, such as a sales receipt or a certificate of authenticity, or a written appraisal of the property.

🗁 THE ESTATE PLANNING DOCUMENT FOLDER

Place your Will and/or Trust in a separate folder. If the original document is in a safe deposit box, then place a copy of the document in this folder together with instructions about how to find the original. If you placed your Will with the Probate Court, then put the address of the Court in the folder together with a copy of the Will.

THE TAX RECORD FOLDER

Your Personal Representative (or next of kin) will need to file your final income tax returns. Keep a copy of your tax returns (both Federal and state) for the past three years in your Tax Record Folder.

CAPITAL GAINS RECORD

As explained in Chapter 2, beginning 2010, there will be a cap on the step-up basis to 4.3 million for property inherited by the spouse and 1.3 million for property inherited by anyone else. It is important to keep a record of the basis of your property, not only for your heirs, but yourself should you decide to sell the property during your lifetime. If you purchase real property, you need to keep a record of the purchase price as well as monies you paid to improve the property. Your accountant can help you set up a bookkeeping system to keep a running record of your basis in everything you own of value.

 THE PERSONAL RECORD FOLDER

The **PERSONAL RECORD FOLDER** should include documents that relate to you personally, such as a birth certificate, naturalization papers, pre-nuptial or post-nuptial agreement, marriage certificate, divorce papers, army records, social security card; etc. If you have an Advance Medical Directive, or a Durable Power of Attorney, then this is a good place for these documents. If you placed the original document in a safe deposit box, then keep a copy in this folder together with the location of the original.

Each folder should contain a record of your ownership of the item and the location of that item. For example, if you own a vacant lot, your beneficiaries will find the deed (or a copy) in your DEED FOLDER, but that deed will not contain the address of that property because it doesn't have one. The post office does not assign a street address until someone actually lives at the site. Your beneficiary could get the location of the property from city or county records. But why make things hard for them, when a simple handwritten note can tell them exactly how to locate the property?

THE *If I Die* FILE

Many do not have the time, nor inclination, to "play" with all these folders. They do not anticipate an immediate demise. Getting hit by a truck, or dying in a fiery plane crash is not something to think about, much less prepare for. But death is not the only problem. You could take suddenly ill (say with a stroke) and become incapacitated. Even the most time-starved optimist should have a murmur of concern that their loved ones will be left with a mess should something unforeseen happen.

If you do not feel like doing a complete job of organizing your records at this time, consider an abridged version. You can set up a single file with a list of all you own and the location of each item. You need to make that file easily accessible to whoever you wish to manage your affairs in the event of your incapacity or death. You can do this by letting that person know of the existence of the file and how to get it in an emergency; or keep the file in an easily accessed place in your home with the succinct but attention-grabbing title of "*If I Die*."

We have included a form on the next page that you can use as a basis for information to be included in the file.

If I Die
then the following information will help settle my estate:

INFORMATION FOR DEATH CERTIFICATE
MY FULL LEGAL NAME _____

MY SOCIAL SECURITY NO. _____

MY USUAL OCCUPATION _____

BIRTH DATE AND BIRTH PLACE _____

If naturalized, date & place _____

MY FATHER'S NAME _____

MY MOTHER'S MAIDEN NAME _____

PERSONS TO BE NOTIFIED OF MY DEATH

_____

_____

_____

FUNERAL AND BURIAL ARRANGEMENTS

LOCATION OF BURIAL SITE

_____

LOCATION OF PRENEED FUNERAL CONTRACT

_____

FOR VETERAN or SPOUSE BURIAL IN A NATIONAL CEMETERY

BRANCH_____SERIAL NO._____
VETERAN'S RANK _____
VETERAN'S VA CLAIM NUMBER _____
DATE AND PLACE OF ENTRY INTO SERVICE:
_____
DATE AND PLACE OF SEPARATION FROM SERVICE:
_____
LOCATION OF OFFICIAL MILITARY DISCHARGE
OR DD 214 FORM_____

LOCATION OF LEGAL DOCUMENTS

BIRTH CERTIFICATE _____

MARRIAGE CERTIFICATE_____

DIVORCE DECREE _____

PASSPORT _____

WILL OR TRUST _____

DEEDS _____

MORTGAGES _____

TITLE TO MOTOR VEHICLES _____

HEALTH CARE DIRECTIVES _____

Name, telephone of attorney   _____

LOCATION OF FINANCIAL RECORDS

INSURANCE POLICIES:

Name of Company, Location of Policy, Insurance Agent

_____

_____

PENSIONS/ANNUITIES:

IF FEDERAL RETIREE: PIN NUMBER: _____

NAME OF SURVIVOR _____

SURVIVOR PIN NUMBER _____

BANK

Name and address of Bank, Account Number,
Location of Safe Deposit Box and Key

_____

_____

SECURITIES

Name and telephone number of broker

_____

TAX RECORDS FOR PAST 3 YEARS

LOCATION _____

Name and telephone number of accountant

_____

WHEN TO UPDATE YOUR ESTATE PLAN

We discussed people's natural disinclination to make an Estate Plan until they are faced with their own mortality. Many believe that they will make just one Will and then die (maybe that's why they put off making a Will). The reality is, most people who make a Will change it at least once before they die. If you have an Estate Plan, it is important to update it when any of the following events take place:

✍ A CHANGE IN RELATIONSHIP

You should examine your Estate Plan on a regular basis to determine whether it needs to be revised. If you decide that your Will needs revision, then it is important to have a new Will prepared. If you simply rip up the old Will, that will effectively revoke the Will. But it could happen that someone (perhaps your attorney) has a copy of the Will. If no one knows that you revoked the Will, they may think the Will is lost and then offer the copy of the Will for Probate (see page 73). If you draft a new Will, then the first paragraph should say, "I revoke all prior Wills ..."

BENEFICIARY MOVES OR DIES

Most people remember to name an alternate beneficiary should a beneficiary die during ones lifetime. But how many of us remember to notify our pension plan or insurance company of a change of address? It is important that your beneficiary's address be available to those in charge of distributing funds upon your death. Many insurance policies are never paid because the company cannot locate the beneficiary. In 1998, the Office of Federal Employees' Group Life Insurance reported that they had 29 million dollars in unpaid benefits, mostly because the beneficiary could not be located at their last given address.

✍ CHANGE IN MARITAL STATUS

If your marry or divorce, there are certain changes that take place by law. For example, if you divorce and then die before you get around to changing your Will or trust, then any provision that you made for your ex-spouse in the document will be read as if your ex-spouse died before you (VA 64.1-59). But it is important to not just rely on the law. Best to change all documents after a divorce or separation. This includes your Advance Medical Directive, Durable Power of Attorney, deeds, insurance policies, etc.

NOTIFY EMPLOYER OF CHANGE IN RELATIONSHIP

If you change your marital status you need to tell your employer of the change so that the employer can change your status for purposes of paycheck withdrawals and health insurance coverage, and change of beneficiary for your Pension Plan.

✍ RELOCATION TO A NEW STATE OR COUNTRY

There is no need to change your Estate Plan for a move within state. If you changed your county of residence and you deposited your original Will with the Clerk of the Circuit Court, then you need to retrieve that Will and deposit it with the Clerk in the county of your new residence. If you move to a new state, then you need to retrieve your Will from the Clerk and take it with you to the new state. Not every state allows the deposit of a Will prior to the death of the Will maker. You may need to make other arrangements to store your Will in the new state. There is much to check out for a move to another state or country. Each state (and country) has its own laws relating to the inheritance of property and those laws are very different from each other. The rights of a spouse to inherit property varies significantly from state to state. There is a world of difference between the rights of a spouse in a community property state and other states. And there is even variation in the rights of a spouse from one community state to another!

If you have a Will or Trust, and you are married, you need to check with an attorney to be sure that your Will or Trust cannot be challenged in the new state because you did not leave your spouse the minimum amount required by the laws of that state.

You also need to check out the taxes of the new state. Each state has its own tax structure. Some states have an inheritance tax, or a transfer tax on all inherited property. If state taxes are high, you may need an Estate Plan that will minimize the impact of those taxes. Creditor protection is another item that is significantly different state to state. If you have much debt, then determine what items can be inherited by your family free of your debts.

Each state has its own, unique, laws of Descent and Distribution. If you do not have a Will, then this is the time to think about who will get your property in the state of your residence. If you have an Advance Medical Directive or Durable Power of Attorney, then you need to determine whether these documents will be honored in the new state. Laws relating to health care vary significantly. Other states may not have a Health Care Agent, but they may have laws that enable you to appoint a Patient Advocate or a Health Care Surrogate with the right to make your health care decisions in the event that you are too ill to do so your-self. It is best to sign a new health care document using the form that is recognized in that state, rather than chance any confusion should you become ill and find yourself in an emergency situation.

If you move to another state or country, it is important to either educate yourself about the laws of the state, or to consult with an attorney who can assist you in reviewing your Estate Plan to see if that plan will accomplish your goals in that state.

✍ A SIGNIFICANT CHANGE IN THE LAW

We pay our legislators (state and federal) to make laws and, if necessary, change those in effect. We pay judges to interpret the law and that interpretation may change the way the law operates. The legislature and the judiciary do their job and so laws change frequently. Tax laws are particularly volatile. The 2001 change in the tax law not only changed income taxes, it significantly increased the exemption amount so that by 2010 no Estate Tax will be due regardless of the value of your Estate. You may be thinking that there is no need for an Estate Tax plan because you don't intend to die prior to 2010. But any certainty relating to death and taxes is false security (especially taxes, in this case). As explained in Chapter 8, the law as passed in 2001, is effective only until December 31, 2010. If lawmakers do nothing, then in 2011, the Federal Estate Tax goes back into effect; and any monies in your estate that exceed one million dollars will be taxable.

And that is not the only uncertainty. Each state has its own Estate Tax structure. It remains to be seen how each state will react to the federal change. Some states may follow the lead of the federal government and increase their Estate Tax exemption in the same manner. Other states may see this as an opportunity to "pick up the slack" i.e., to increase their Estate Taxes, so that monies that would have been paid to the federal government will now be paid to the state.

You need to keep up with the news to learn about changes in the law that affect your Estate Plan. It is a good idea to check with your attorney on a regular basis to see if any change in the state or federal law affects your current Estate plan. And also visit the Eagle Publishing Company Web site for changes we will post to keep this book fresh:

http://www.eaglepublishing.com

GAMES DECEDENTS PLAY

We discussed the game of "hide and seek" some decedents play with their heirs. A variation of that game is the "wild goose chase." The person who plays this game is one who never updates his files. His records are filled with all sorts of lapsed insurance policies, promissory notes of debts long since paid; brokerage statements of securities that have been sold, and so on.

When he is gone, his family will become frustrated as they try to hunt down the "missing" asset. If you wish to play this game, then the best joke is to keep the key to a safe deposit box that you are no longer leasing. That will keep folks hunting for a long time!

If you do not have a wicked sense of humor, then do your family a favor and update your records on a regular basis.

Glossary

ABSTRACT An *abstract* of an Affidavit is a short, abbreviated summary of the information contained in the document.

ADMINISTRATION The *administration* of a Probate Estate is the management and settlement of the decedent's affairs. There are different types of administration. See *Ancillary Administration.*

ADVANCE MEDICAL DIRECTIVE An *Advance Medical Directive* is a statement made by someone in the presence of witnesses or a written, notarized statement in which the person gives directions about the care he/she wishes to receive in the event he/she is too ill to direct his/her treatment. The Advance Medical Directive could contain a Living Will or an appointment of someone to act as the principal's Health Care Agent.

AFFIANT An *affiant* is someone who signs an affidavit and swears or acknowledges that it is true in the presence of a Notary Public or other person with authority to administer an oath or take acknowledgments.

AFFIDAVIT An *affidavit* is a written statement of fact made by someone voluntarily, under oath, or acknowledged as being true, in the presence of a notary public or someone else who has authority to administer an oath or take acknowledgments.

AGENT An *agent* is someone who is authorized by another (the principal) to act for or in place of the principal.

ANATOMICAL GIFT An *anatomical gift* is the donation of all or part of the body of the decedent for a specified purpose, such as transplantation or research.

ANCILLARY ADMINISTRATION An *ancillary administration* is a probate procedure that aids or assists the original (primary) probate proceeding. Ancillary administration is conducted in another state to determine the beneficiary of the decedent's property located within that state, and to determine whether the property is taxable in that state.

ANNUITANT   An *annuitant* is someone who is entitled to receive payments under an annuity contract.

ANNUITY An *annuity* is a contract that gives someone (the annuitant) the right to receive periodic payments (monthly, quarterly) either for life or for a number of years.

ASSET An *asset* is anything owned by someone that has a value, including personal property (jewelry, paintings, securities, cash, motor vehicles, etc.) and real property (condominiums, vacant lots, acreage, residences, etc.)

BASIS   The *basis* is a value that is assigned to an asset for the purpose of determining the gain (or loss) on the sale of the item or in determining the value of the item in the hands of someone who has received it as a gift.

BENEFICIARY A *beneficiary* is one who benefits from the act of another or from the transfer of property. In this book we refer to a beneficiary as someone named in a Will or Trust to receive property, or someone who inherits property under the Laws of Intestate Succession.

CAPITAL GAINS TAX   A *Capital Gains tax* is a tax on the increase in the basis of property sold by a taxpayer.

CAVEAT   *Caveat* is Latin for "Let him beware." It is a warning for the reader to be careful.

CHARITABLE REMAINDER ANNUITY TRUST   A *Charitable Remainder Annuity Trust* is a Trust that is required to pay an annuity to a designated person for a certain period of time. Once the annuity is paid, whatever remains in the Trust is donated to a tax exempt charity.

CIRCUIT A *circuit* is a judicial division. The state of Virginia is divided into 31 judicial circuits each with its own Circuit Court. Each county has a Circuit Court. Many cities, such as Alexandria, Charlottesville, Fredericksburg, Richmond and Salem have their own Circuit Court.

CLAIM A *claim* against the decedent's estate is a demand for payment of a debt of the decedent. To be effective, the claim must be filed with the Probate court within the time limits set by law.

CODE A *code* is a body of laws arranged systematically for easy reference e.g. the Internal Revenue Code and the Code of Virginia.

CODICIL A *Codicil* to a Will is supplement or an addition to a Will that changes certain parts of the Will.

COLUMBARIUM A *Columbarium* is a vault with niches (spaces) for urns that contain the ashes of cremated bodies.

COMMISSIONER OF ACCOUNTS The *Commissioner of Accounts* is someone appointed by the Judge of a Circuit Court to supervise those who are appointed as a fiduciary (Personal Representative, Guardian, Trustee, etc.) by the Court. Each year the fiduciary must file an accounting with the Commissioner (VA 26-8).

COMMON LAW MARRIAGE A *Common Law marriage* is one that is entered into without a state marriage license nor any kind of official marriage ceremony. A common law marriage is created by an agreement to marry, followed by the two living together as man and wife. Most states do not recognize a common law marriage.

CONSERVATOR A *Conservator* is a person appointed by the Court to care for the property of someone who is unable to do so himself.

COURT The *Court* as used in this book is the Circuit Court. When referring to an order made by the court then the term is synonymous with "Judge," i.e., an "order of the court" is an order made by the Judge of the Circuit Court.

CREMAINS The word *cremains* is an abbreviation of the term *cremated remains*. It is also referred to as the *ashes* of a person who has been cremated.

CURTESY *Curtesy* is the right of a husband, upon the death of his wife, to a life estate in any real property she owned during their marriage, provided they had a surviving child who could inherit the property. This English Common Law has been abolished in most state.

DECEDENT The *decedent* is the person who died.

DESCENDANT A *descendant* is someone who descends from a common ancestor. There are two kinds of descendants: a *lineal descendant* and a *collateral descendant*. The lineal descendant is one who descends in a straight line such as father to son to grandson. The collateral descendant is one who descends in a parallel line, such as a cousin. In this book, unless otherwise stated, the term *descendant* refers to a *lineal descendant*.

DISTRIBUTION The *distribution* of a Trust estate or of a Probate Estate is the transfer to a beneficiary that part of the estate to which the beneficiary is entitled.

DOWER *Dower* is the Common Law right of a wife, upon the death of her husband, to a life estate in 1/3rd of all property owned by her husband during their marriage. Most states, including Virginia have abolished the law.

DURABLE POWER OF ATTORNEY A *Durable Power of Attorney* is a document in which the person who signs the document (the *Principal*) gives another person (his *Agent* or *Attorney in Fact*) authority to do certain things on behalf of the Principal. The word *"durable"* means that the authority of the Agent continues even if the Principal is incapacitated at the time that the Agent is acting on behalf of the Principal.

EQUITABLE *Equitable* is whatever is right or just. If property is distributed to two or more people equitably, then the division is not necessarily equal, but according to the principles of justice or fairness.

ESTATE A person's *Estate* is all of the property (both real and personal property) owned by that person. The decedent's estate may also be referred to as his *Taxable Estate* because all of the decedent's assets must be included when determining whether any Estate taxes are due after the person dies. Compare to Probate Estate.

EXECUTOR An *Executor* is someone appointed by a Will maker to carry out the directions and requests in his Will.

FIDUCIARY A *Fiduciary* is one who holds property in trust for another or one who acts for the benefit of another, such as a Personal Representative, trustee, guardian, conservator, etc.

GRANTEE The *Grantee* named in a deed is the person who receives title to the property from the grantor.

GRANTOR A *Grantor* is someone who transfers property. The grantor of a deed is the person who transfers property to a new owner (the *Grantee*). The grantor of a trust is someone who creates the trust and then transfer's property into the trust. See *Settlor*.

GUARDIAN A *Guardian* is someone who has legal authority to care for the person or property of a minor or for someone who has been found by the court to be incapacitated.

HEALTH CARE AGENT A *Health Care Agent* is someone who is appointed under an Advance Medical Directive to make medical decisions for another (the *Principal)* in the event that the Principal is too ill to make those decisions for himself.

HEIR An *heir* is anyone entitled to inherit the decedent's property under the Laws of Descent and Distribution in the event that the decedent dies without a Will.

HOMESTEAD The *homestead* is the dwelling and land owned and occupied as the owner's principal residence.

INCAPACITATED The term *incapacitated* is used in two ways. A person is *physically incapacitated* if he lacks the ability to care for himself in some way. A person is *legally incapacitated* if a court finds that a person is unable to care for his person or property. Once the Court determines that a person is legally incapacitated, the judge will appoint someone to care for person or property of the incapacitated person.

INDIGENT A person who is *indigent* is one who is poor and without funds.

INTER VIVOS TRUST   An *Inter Vivos Trust* (also known as a *Living Trust*) is Trust that is created and becomes effective during the lifetime of the Settlor (or Grantor) as contrasted with a Trust that the Settlor includes as part of his Will to take effective upon his death.

INTESTATE   *Intestate* means not having a Will or dying without a Will. *Testate* is to have a Will or dying with a Will.

IRREVOCABLE CONTRACT   An *irrevocable contract* is a contract that cannot be revoked, withdrawn, or cancelled by any of the parties to that contract.

JOINT AND SEVERAL LIABILITY   If two or more people agree to be *jointly and severally liable* to pay a debt, then each individually agree to be responsible to pay the debt, and together they all agree to pay for the debt.

KEY MAN INSURANCE   *Key man insurance* is an insurance policy designed to protect a company from economic loss in the event that an important employee of the company becomes disabled or dies.

LEGALESE   *Legalese* refers to the use of legal terms and confusing text that is used by many attorneys to draft legal documents.

LETTERS   *Letters* is a document, issued by the Probate court, giving the Personal Representative authority to take possession of and to administer the estate of the decedent.

LIEN   A *lien* is a charge against a person's property as security for a debt. The lien is evidence of the creditor's right to take the property as full or partial payment, in the event that the debtor defaults in paying the monies owed.

LIFE ESTATE A *Life Estate* interest in real property is the right to possess and occupy that property for so long as the holder of the life estate lives.

LINEAL DESCENDANT A *lineal descendant* of the decedent is someone who is his direct descendant, such as his child, grandchild, great-grandchild etc.

LITIGATION   *Litigation* is the process of carrying on a lawsuit, i.e., to sue for some right or remedy in a court of law. A Litigation Attorney is one who is experienced in conducting the law suit and in particular, going to trial.

LIVING WILL   A *Living Will* is a legal document that gives instructions about whether life support systems should be withheld in the event that the person who signs the Living Will is terminally ill or in a persistent vegetative state and unable to speak for himself.

MEDICAID   *Medicaid* is a public assistance program that is sponsored jointly by the federal and state government to provide medical care for people with low income and little assets

NET PROCEEDS The *net proceeds* of a sale is the sale price less costs and expenses paid to make the sale.

NET WORTH A person's *net worth* is the value of all of the property that he owns less the monies he owes.

NEXT OF KIN   *Next of kin* has two meanings in law: *next of kin* can refer to a person's nearest blood relation or it can refer to those people (not necessarily blood relations) who are entitled to inherit the property of the decedent if the decedent died without a will.

PERJURY *Perjury* is lying under oath. The false statement can be made as a witness in court or by signing an Affidavit. Perjury is a criminal offense.

PERSONAL PROPERTY *Personal property* is all property owned by a person that is not real property (real estate). It includes cars, stocks, house furnishings, jewelry, etc.

PERSONAL REPRESENTATIVE   A *Personal Representative* is someone who is appointed by the Probate court to settle the decedent's estate and to distribute whatever is left to the proper beneficiary.

PER STIRPES *Per Stirpes* is a method of distributing property to a group of people such that if one of them dies before the gift is made, then that deceased person's share goes to his/her descendants.

PETITION A *petition* is a formal written request to a Court asking the Court to take action or issue an order on a given matter.

POST-NUPTIAL AGREEMENT A *Post-nuptial agreement* is an agreement made by a couple after marriage to decide their respective rights in case of a dissolution or the death of a spouse

POWER OF ATTORNEY A *Power of Attorney* is a document in which the person who signs the document (the *Principal*) gives another person (his *Agent*) authority to do certain things on behalf of the Principal.

PRE-NUPTIAL AGREEMENT A *Pre-nuptial agreement* (also known as an *Antenuptial agreement*) is an agreement made prior to marriage whereby a couple determines how their property is to be managed during their marriage and how their property is to be divided should one die, or they later divorce.

PROBATE   *Probate* is a court procedure in which a court determines the existence of a valid Will and then supervises the distribution of the Probate Estate of the decedent.

PROBATE ESTATE   The *Probate Estate* is that part of the decedent's estate that is subject to probate. It includes property that the decedent owned in his name only. It does not include property that was jointly held by the decedent and someone else. It does not include property held "in trust for" or "for the benefit of" someone.

PUNITIVE DAMAGES *Punitive damages* are monies awarded to a victim, by a court, to punish the wrongdoer for the malicious and willful acts that he committed against the victim.

REAL PROPERTY   *Real property*, also known as *real estate*, is land and anything permanently attached to the land such as buildings and fences.

REGISTERED AGENT   A *Registered Agent* of a corporation is someone who is authorized to act on behalf of the company and accept service of process in the event the company is sued.

RESIDUARY BENEFICIARY   A *residuary beneficiary* is a beneficiary named in a Will who is to receive all or part of whatever is left of the Probate Estate once the specific gifts made in the Will have been distributed and after the decedent's bills, taxes and costs of probate have been paid.

RESIDUARY ESTATE   A *Residuary Estate* is that part of a probate estate that is left after all expenses and costs of administration have been paid and specific gifts have been distributed.

SETTLOR   A *Settlor* is someone who furnishes property that is placed in a Trust. If the Settlor is also the creator of the Trust, then the settlor is also referred to as the Grantor.

SPENDTHRIFT   A *Spendthrift* is someone who spends money carelessly or wastefully or extravagantly.

SPENDTHRIFT TRUST   A *Spendthrift Trust* is a Trust created to provide monies to a beneficiary, and at the same time protect the Trust property from being taken by the creditors of the beneficiary.

STEP-UP BASIS   A *step-up basis* is the value placed on property that is acquired in a taxable transaction (such as inheriting property) or in a purchase (IRC 1012). The "step-up" refers to the increase in value of basis, from the basis of former owner (usually what he paid for it), to the basis of the new owner (usually the market value when the transfer is made).

STATUTE OF LIMITATION   A *Statute of Limitation* is a federal or state law that sets maximum time periods for taking legal action. Once the time set out in the statute passes, no legal action can be taken.

TAX EXLUSION   A *tax exclusion* is income that is not taxed because of a Internal Revenue Code provision.

TENANCY BY THE ENTIRETY   A *Tenancy by the Entirety* is the name of a form of ownership of real property held by a husband and wife. It has the same legal effect as a joint tenancy with right of survivorship.

TENANCY IN COMMON   *Tenancy in common* is a form of ownership such that each tenant owns his/her share without any claim to that share by the other tenants. Unlike a joint tenancy, there is no right of survivorship. Once a tenant in common dies, his/her share belongs to the tenant's estate and not to the remaining owners of the property.

TESTATE   *Testate* means having a Will or dying with a Will.

TITLE INSURANCE   *Title Insurance* is a policy issued by a title company after searching title to the property. The policy insures the accuracy of the title search against a claim of a defective title.

TRUST AGREEMENT A *Trust agreement* is document in which someone (the Grantor or Trustor) creates a Trust and appoints a Trustee to manage property placed into the trust. The usual purpose of the Trust is to benefit persons or charities named by the Grantor as beneficiaries of the Trust.

TRUSTEE   A *Trustee* is a person, or institution, who accepts the duty of caring for property for the benefit of another.

UNDUE INFLUENCE   *Undue influence* is pressure, influence or persuasion that overpowers a person's free will or judgment, so that a person acts according to the will or purpose of the dominating party.

WAIVER   A *waiver* is the intentional and voluntary giving up of a known right.

WARD   A *Ward* is a minor or an incapacitated person who is placed by the Court under the care and supervision of a Guardian or a Conservator..

WARRANTY DEED   A *warranty deed* is a deed in which someone (the Grantor) transfers the property to another (the Grantee) and guarantees good title, i.e., the Grantor guarantees that he has the right to transfer the property, and that no one else has any right to the property.

WRONGFUL DEATH   A *wrongful death* is a death that was caused by the willful or negligent act of a person or company.

INDEX

196 Virginia Statutes are referenced in
Guiding Those Left Behind In Virginia

Each state has its own set of laws relating to the settlement of a person's estate. The Virginia laws that are referenced in this book are very different from the laws of other states. The author is in now in the process of "translating" *Guiding Those Left Behind*... for the rest of the states; that is, to write a book that incorporates the laws of the state into a book that describes how to settle the affairs of a decedent in that state, and how to prepare an estate plan that is appropriate for the state.

Alabama, Arizona, California, Florida, Georgia, Indiana, Illinois, Maryland, Massachusetts, Michigan, Minnesota, Missouri, New Jersey, New York, North Carolina, Ohio, Pennsylvania, South Carolina, Tennessee, Texas, Virginia, Wisconsin and Washington are now in print.

The following books are scheduled for release in 2002:
Guiding Those Left Behind In Colorado
Guiding Those Left Behind In Kentucky
Guiding Those Left Behind In Louisiana
Guiding Those Left Behind In Mississippi

To order a book call (800) 824-0823.
Visit our Web site http://www.eaglepublishing.com
to check whether books for other states are available at this time.

Beyond Grief To Acceptance and Peace

AMELIA E. POHL and the noted psychologist BARBARA J. SIMMONDS, Ph.d, have written a book for those families who have suffered a loss.

Beyond Grief To Acceptance and Peace explains:
- ◇ What to say to the bereaved
- ◇ How to help a child through the loss
- ◇ Strategies to adjust to a new life style
- ◇ When and where to seek assistance.

The second edition of this 80 page book is now available for $9.95 plus shipping and handling. You can order the book using the following discount coupon for a total of $9.

DISCOUNT COUPON

Please send me a copy of Beyond Grief To Acceptance and Peace

☐ I am enclosing a check for $9.
☐ Charge this to my _____ credit card
(Visa, Master, etc.)
Credit Card no. _____
Expiration date: _____

Name _____
Address _____
_____

Mail this coupon to:
EAGLE PUBLISHING COMPANY OF BOCA
4199 N. Dixie Hwy. #2
Boca Raton, FL   33431

It is the goal of EAGLE PUBLISHING COMPANY to keep our publications fresh.

As we receive information about changes to the federal or Virginia law we will post an update to this edition at our Web site:

http://www.eaglepublishing.com